RESISTANCE IN THE BLUEGRASS

RESISTANCE IN THE BLUEGRASS

EMPOWERING THE COMMONWEALTH

FARRAH ALEXANDER

FOREWORD BY REPRESENTATIVE ATTICA SCOTT

 UNIVERSITY PRESS OF KENTUCKY

Published by The University Press of Kentucky,
scholarly publisher for the Commonwealth, serving
Bellarmine University, Berea College, Centre College of
Kentucky, Eastern Kentucky University, The Filson Historical
Society, Georgetown College, Kentucky Historical Society,
Kentucky State University, Morehead State University,
Murray State University, Northern Kentucky University,
Spalding University, Transylvania University, University of
Kentucky, University of Louisville, and Western Kentucky University.
All rights reserved.

Editorial and Sales Offices: The University Press of Kentucky
663 South Limestone Street, Lexington, Kentucky 40508-4008
www.kentuckypress.com

Cataloging-in-Publication data available from the Library of Congress

ISBN 978-0-8131-9526-1 (hardcover: alk. paper)
ISBN 978-0-8131-8720-4 (pbk.: alk. paper)
ISBN 978-0-8131-8721-1 (pdf)
ISBN 978-0-8131-8722-8 (epub)

This book is printed on acid-free paper meeting the requirements
of the American National Standard for Permanence in
Paper for Printed Library Materials.

∞

Manufactured in the United States of America.

Member of the Association of University Presses

ASSOCIATION
of UNIVERSITY
PRESSES

TO THE TIRELESS KENTUCKIAN
CHANGE MAKERS WHO HAVE BLESSED ME
WITH THE HONOR OF TELLING THEIR STORIES

In every age, no matter how cruel the oppression carried on by those in power, there have been those who struggled for a different world. I believe this is the genius of humankind, the thing that makes us half divine: the fact that some human beings can envision a world that has never existed.
Anne Braden

CONTENTS

Foreword by Representative Attica Scott ix

Introduction 1

1. Poverty 5

2. Environment 35

3. Religion 59

4. Education 87

5. Political Representation 111

6. Racial Justice 143

7. LGBTQ+ Rights 169

8. Immigration 193

9. Feminism and Reproductive Rights 213

Acknowledgments 231

Source Notes 233

Suggested Reading 239

Index 245

FOREWORD

RESISTANCE IN THE BLUEGRASS is a complementary book to author Farrah Alexander's *Raising the Resistance: A Mother's Guide to Practical Activism*.

In *Resistance in the Bluegrass*, readers are taken on a journey through what has always been a part of what makes Kentucky home for many of us—resistance—whether occupying the railroad tracks in Harlan, Kentucky, and chanting, "No pay, we stay!" or occupying Injustice Square Park in downtown Louisville and chanting, "No justice, no peace!"

We are Kentucky—the ones who marched in Appalachia for Black lives, and the ones who showed up in western Kentucky to end poverty.

We are Kentucky—the ones who resist corporate control over our lives, and the ones who are creating the care communities across the commonwealth.

We are Kentucky—the ones who are protecting our environment, and the ones who know that healthcare is a human right.

Our own bell hooks reminds us: "True resistance begins with people confronting pain . . . and wanting to do something to change it."

That is our story. It is who we are at our core. Rather than linger in our pain, we resist any notions of giving up, of throwing in the towel, of walking away from a challenge. We certainly know about challenges in Kentucky. We know what it means to be displaced from our mobile home communities. We know what it means not to have clean bathing and drinking water. We know the sting of discrimination based on who we love. We also know what community, love, and solidarity look like in action.

Kentucky has a deep civil rights history. That history has helped shape the human rights and social justice movements of today, whether it was the history of open housing advocacy, creation of the Fairness Campaign, or public school desegregation. We have learned valuable lessons from the movements of our parents and grand-parents. Today, we join our neighbors who are showing up for racial justice, who are fighting for fairness, and who are centering disability rights. We may not all be in this together, but we will certainly get there together.

Tomorrow, our children will forge a future that is beyond our wildest dreams—a future that is built on community, love, and solidarity. In that future is a new and different kind of political representation. It is one that is born from a place of abundance—a place that values justice and the perspectives of young people, women, and people from different ethnic and racial backgrounds. We can get there. We can get to the place where we are all valued and loved for who we are and how we show up in the world. It is a big and bold vision of our future that we each deserve. We cannot settle. We are worthy of everything.

Resistance in the Bluegrass includes building a more representative democracy. We have been fired up across the commonwealth as people who come from where we come from, and who share our life stories and lived experiences.

Some of us are putting it all on the line to change the face of Kentucky politics, despite the barriers, despite the odds that are stacked against us. There is vulnerability in that place. There is sacrifice in that place. There is joy in that place. And there is true resistance in that place. Resistance to the way things were. Resistance to normal. Resistance to the establishment. Resistance to the status quo. Resistance to and rejection of the politics of exclusion and marginalization. Instead, we are hollering for all to hear that Kentucky is our home and we belong here.

As a mama in the Bluegrass, I have always wanted my children to know that they belong here. It makes a difference when our children see themselves reflected in every aspect of the societies that we are creating. It makes a difference when we raise our children to resist ableism, ageism, racism, sexism, and all of the -isms. Motherhood and parenting are a form of resistance for me. I have taught my children that we do not move in fear. My daughter and I have faced down tear gas and have been unjustly arrested just because we believe in police accountability and reject the carceral state. I have taught my children that we must not bow down to institutional and systemic racism. We are worthy of so much more.

Our children must be taught to reject the notion that maleness and whiteness must be centered above all else. That is violence. That is silence. That is erasure. We can raise children who are so confident in themselves that they have absolutely no interest in, nor time for, elevating themselves above anyone else. Our children can be everything they dream of being without oppressing anyone in order to achieve their goals. We have a responsibility to raise children who will build a better world for all of us—not just some of us.

As you read *Resistance in the Bluegrass*, reflect on your own form of resistance. What are you building? How are you building? Who is part of your community? Where do you show up?

We can build together by making sure that our basic human needs are being met. We can create inclusive and welcoming communities. We can show up through action and advocacy.

This is community. This is what a caring community looks like. We take care of one another. We dismantle the barriers and gaps that can prevent people and families from being whole. We take care of ourselves. One of the bravest forms of resistance is caring for yourself when the world tells you that you must do more, do too much, or do the most.

Reading was and continues to be an act of resistance. My ancestors were beaten and mutilated for learning how to read. Reading remains fundamental to our collective liberation. It is how we rise. It is how we create transformational change. It is how we build the beloved community.

State Representative Attica Scott

INTRODUCTION

WHEN DESCRIBING what the Commonwealth of Kentucky is most known for, you may suggest the Kentucky Derby or Kentucky Fried Chicken. At least, that's what an Irishman in Dublin did when I said I was from Kentucky. You may not instantly think of power.

This is a persistent underestimate of the Bluegrass. Too often Kentucky is dismissed as a flyover state (hello, we're a flyover *commonwealth*!) or just a block of red on an electoral map of votes. Historically, Kentuckians have made vast contributions to our nation's political landscape. In the early 1800s, Senator and Secretary of State Henry Clay represented Kentucky and influenced diplomatic policy by pioneering the war hawk philosophy. You likely can't watch cable news for more than thirty minutes without seeing Senator Mitch McConnell, who has been representing Kentucky longer than I have been alive.

You may not agree with the war hawkish philosophy that brought us such resounding successes as the Iraq War and Vietnam. You may have donated money to Amy McGrath's campaign, not necessarily because you supported her platform so strongly, but because you would support literally anyone running against Mitch McConnell. But right here in Kentucky, he wields serious political power.

Throughout the years, political activists in Kentucky have also demonstrated serious power. But for many of them, it wasn't until decades later that their legacies and contributions were realized. As I learned more about Kentuckians' contributions to activism, I found myself frequently awed by the courage and vision they demonstrated.

Inside you'll hear the incredible story of Anne Braden, who shook up segregated housing practices, practiced antiracism, and was praised for her actions in Martin Luther King Jr.'s *Letter from Birmingham Jail*. You'll learn about Ira Grupper, who began his activism journey in the historic Student Nonviolent Coordinating Committee alongside icons like John Lewis, and who now spouts Yiddish swearwords while lamenting that he can't take to the streets alongside others protesting racial injustice. You'll meet Taylor Ryan, who built a groundbreaking nonprofit and mutual aid network meeting the needs of the Black community and spreading unapologetic joy.

These activists have shaped and continue to shape our political landscape and help make the commonwealth a more just and equitable place for all Kentuckians. They're extraordinary people with fascinating stories and a vision for the future of Kentucky. But what is really extraordinary is that they're . . . just ordinary. So many of the featured activists manifested the change they wished to see only with a vision and passion to make it happen.

I hope that, as you read their stories, you'll feel as inspired and hopeful as I did.

ONE

POVERTY

COUNTRY SINGER Loretta Lynn once sang of her old Kentucky home, "Well, I was born'd a coal miner's daughter, in a cabin on a hill in Butcher Holler." The cabin, still sitting in a lush landscape of bluegrass in eastern Kentucky, features distressed wood, but not the kind Joanna Gaines might fawn over, more the type that looks like it may crumble any minute. In the decades since Lynn wrote those words, much has stayed the same, preserved like her hometown cabin, and yet much has changed.

The coal mines, one of the largest industries in the commonwealth, were once a reliable source of income for many Kentuckians, a way of providing for families like Lynn sings of with a sense of pride and fondness. But the work of a coal miner is difficult and dangerous. It is not only hard work—physically demanding—it carries serious consequences for the miner's health. Black lung disease, the lingering, debilitating condition formally known as pneumoconiosis, is a common result of the inhalation of coal dust. Coal mining remains one of the most dangerous occupations an American can have, with between sixty and seventy miners dying annually from disasters or disease.

Throughout the hollers of rural Kentucky, many of the coal mines are now closed. Widespread areas such as Daniel Boone National Forest feature awe-inspiring natural bridges, stunning sunsets, gorgeous waterfalls—and devastating poverty. Many of the counties on the southern, eastern, and western borders of Kentucky, which once boasted legions of coal miners, now top published lists like USA Today's "Worst Counties to Live In." The newspaper analyzed such factors as poverty, education, and life expectancy to pinpoint the least desirable places for Americans to live. Of the twenty-five counties that made the list, ten were in Kentucky. The once reliable and now drastically declining coal industry is often identified as a likely culprit, as the counties suffering such widespread poverty are also counties once home to booming mines.

At Cumberland Falls, sometimes known as the Niagara of the South, truly gorgeous waterfalls sit hidden among hiking trails and forests in McCreary County on the southern edge of the commonwealth. The county is also the poorest, not only in the commonwealth but in the entire country. It is the only county where most households earn less than $20,000 per year. About 10.5 percent of Americans meet the criteria for living in poverty, but in McCreary County the figure is 34.5 percent.

Across Appalachia, Kentuckians disproportionately live below the poverty line. The Appalachian region, comprising parts of Alabama, Kentucky, Tennessee, Virginia, and West Virginia, has a higher rate of poverty than the average in the United States. But even within Appalachia, Kentucky boasts a still higher rate. For example, between 2010 and 2014, about 19.7 percent of Appalachians lived in poverty, which is disproportionately higher than the rest of the country. But Kentucky specifically had a 25.4 percent rate, compared to 18.9 percent in the rest of the Appalachian region.

When you consider these figures and see the areas of Appalachian Kentucky with the dilapidated mobile homes, long food pantry lines, and abandoned coal mines, you may come to the usual conclusion. Coal mines provided many Kentuckians with jobs. The coal mines closed. The people, now jobless, live in poverty.

The truth is a bit more nuanced. First of all, coal mining jobs are not quite as illustrious as in the Loretta Lynn days. Decades back, many coal miners were unionized. Just two decades ago, more than 40 percent of the coal mining jobs were unionized. But by 2016, only 2.5 percent were unionized. This can make a big difference, as the United Mine Workers of America boasts that the average unionized miner can earn at least $61,650 annually and up to $85,000 with overtime.

Although the work is undeniably hard and risky, a $60K+ job without the requirement of a college degree is extremely appealing to many Kentuckians. It's what I've personally heard my grandparents, who grew up poor in the commonwealth, refer to with raised eyebrows as "good money." That's what the coal mines meant to many, "good money," an opportunity to provide for your family, purchase a house. Yes, of course, the possibility of death is indeed much higher than if you chose nearly any other career, but . . . good money.

The money now is simply not as good, as the jobs have become harder to find. Employers are offering temporary jobs, few benefits, and only $17 an hour or so. It's enough to still draw Kentuckians in, but without permanent positions, many find themselves cycling through getting a temporary job, being laid off, and repeating the process many times. The income instability is compounded by the lack of benefits such as health insurance in an occupation where the significant health risks can be financially devastating.

Meanwhile, the pay disparity among positions in coal mining companies is vast. At the time of this writing, there is a coal mining position available in eastern Kentucky offering an annual income of $28,000. The average executive salary at that same company is $218,000 per year. It's no surprise that coal companies are suffering, many closing mines and filing for bankruptcy. But the companies often still pay their executives millions throughout the process. Alpha Natural Resources, a large coal producer based in Pike County, Kentucky, gradually scaled back operations until they finally closed their last Kentucky coal mine in 2016, costing 117 miners their jobs. That same year, the company gave their executives a $12 million bonus package during the bankruptcy proceedings following losses of $1.3 billion. The company's reasoning? The executives deserved to be compensated for navigating the difficult process.

It would make sense that the high number of Kentuckians in poverty would correlate with a high unemployment rate, but that's not exactly the case. The unemployment rate in Kentucky is comparable with the rest of the United States. Before the COVID-19 pandemic, the unemployment rate in the country was 6.3 percent. When we look at unemployment in McCreary County, Kentucky—which, remember, is the poorest county in the entire United States—it is only 6.2 percent, even lower than average.

This may seem unfathomable, but a county with nearly 94 percent of the population employed and more than one-third living in poverty is undeniably an example of the working poor. The struggle of the working poor is not just living paycheck to paycheck, it's having those paychecks not cover basic needs. Many Kentuckians are working the same jobs once reliably known for "good money" and yet struggling to feed their families or provide housing for themselves.

Living in Pandemic Conditions All the Time

Now living in Louisville with his family, Ben Carter grew up in Lexington and later in Russell, near Ashland. As he says the word "Ashland," I feel a rush of warm nostalgia for a city I've never even visited. While coal may have been the big industry for job security in previous generations, for millennials like Ben and me, it was a booming oil and gas industry.

I vividly recall the blue and red Ashland logo on my grandpa's work shirts as he'd return home on the weekends. For blue-collar workers like my grandpa, the jobs at places like Ashland were more than appealing, they were practically answered prayers. My grandpa worked at the eastern Kentucky company, three hours away from his home and family, and rented the smallest, cheapest apartment he could find nearby, just to have a place to sleep after a long day so he could do it again the next. Ashland Oil eventually faced the same fate as many coal mines in the commonwealth. But despite the logistic difficulties, my family still spoke of Ashland fondly and gratefully, years after its closure.

When Ben Carter recalls growing up near Ashland, he seems to share similar warm, nostalgic feelings associated with living near the rare booming rural industry. He describes his high school as being one of the best in the commonwealth, even compared to such standouts as Manual and some of the private Catholic schools. Knowing that I want to talk to him about poverty and his work to combat it, he reflects, saying that he's sure there *was* poverty, but growing up he didn't see it much.

He sees it now.

Today Carter works as Senior Litigation and Advocacy Counsel for the Kentucky Equal Justice Center, which is a poverty law advocacy center. In advocating for low-income Kentuckians, the issues the nonprofit tackles are vast—everything from nursing home violations to wage abuses to human trafficking. It seems KEJC understands the nuances of Kentucky poverty and the tangled web of bureaucracy behind it, which the Center does its best to unweave.

Since the COVID-19 pandemic began, Carter has been actively advocating for housing justice, helping tenants fight evictions. Kentucky, like many states across the country, enacted an eviction moratorium not allowing landlords to evict tenants. When tenants are unable to pay rent, however, it's not as simple as the amount owed being forgiven. The tenants still must pay the rent owed, even if they're unable. While the pandemic brought some of these issues to the forefront, Ben Carter knows that neither low-income Kentuckians nor their struggles are completely new.

"A lot of people are in pandemic conditions all the time, whether they can't go to work because we have a stay-at-home order or whether they can't go to work because of systemic racism or the skills that they have are no longer marketable because surface mining of coal is no longer a thing that there's a market for," says Carter. "There are all sorts of people who can't go to work under normal circumstances, whether it's workplace disability or sexual harassment or whatever it might be."

One of the big issues that Carter tackles, one that faces the working poor as well, is wage theft. The need to address this issue became evident from much of the work done at the Maxwell Street Legal Clinic in Lexington, a KEJC program that specifically helps the immigrant population, who often fall through the cracks of the justice system otherwise. Many immigrants who first came to the clinic for immigration assistance were soon asking questions about wage theft and what rights they had to make their employers pay what was owed.

Wage theft is extremely common and widespread. Every year, employers take billions from their employees' paychecks by denying them earned tips and overtime pay, asking them to work off the clock, and other unlawful practices. These violations affect 17 percent of low-wage workers, who can least afford to lose earnings. Wage theft often pushes workers below the poverty line, forcing them to rely on public assistance even if they hadn't before. So wage theft not only affects the working poor but also costs taxpayer money, puts pressure on state and local economies, and hurts other workers through its downward pressure on wages.

Those who seek legal aid from the Maxwell Street Legal Clinic are unfortunately likely victims of wage theft. They're working for low wages and aren't likely to be in a position to fight back as they're simultaneously fighting immigration-related issues. Wage theft is best combatted with state legal protections, increased penalties for violators, and protection for workers against retaliation when wage theft is reported. The vulnerable workers seeking legal aid may not have the resources to fight for those protections, but KEJC does.

With the onset of the COVID-19 pandemic, as many Kentuckians found themselves working from home or not working at all, issues such as housing justice and an eviction crisis suddenly became more widely discussed along with the wistful notion of "getting back to normal." But as Carter sees it, these issues are normal for many low-income Kentuckians facing crisis after crisis.

James Baldwin once said, "Anyone who has ever struggled with poverty knows how extremely expensive it is to be poor." Carter and others in the Kentucky Equal Justice Center see evidence of this all the time. A single unexpected medical bill financially devastates some Kentucky families. Most are much closer to homelessness than to financial independence. Poor Kentuckians are indebted to poverty and constantly paying the interest in the form of stolen wages, collections, late fees, predatory rates, and so on.

"People want to go back to normal, right?" says Carter. "They're so desperate to go back to normal. But normal was not OK for large swaths of our neighbors. Under normal circumstances, forty percent of Americans don't have four hundred dollars in savings to deal with an emergency in their budget. Seventy-eight percent of African American people in Kentucky have some sort of debt in collections and half of that is medical debt, and the numbers are not much better for white Kentuckians.

"I feel proud that we are working on policies that actually help people in a pandemic, but it's like people are in pandemic conditions all the time."

While Ben Carter and the nonprofits like the Kentucky Equal Justice Center fight the policies and bureaucracy that keep poor people down in Kentucky, there still exists an immediate need that sometimes nonprofits and even highly regulated food pantries can't address. In those moments of crisis, people need help right away. They may want policy change and systemic change, but those changes won't pay their electric bills before the power is turned off or put food in their empty refrigerators. For those needs, many poor Kentuckians find themselves relying on each other through grassroots mutual aid networks.

No One Goes Without in a Trailer Park

Mutual aid is a concept and practice that has existed in some form perhaps forever. For self-preservation and survival, people take responsibility to care for one another. Participants collaborate to find strategies and resources to meet each other's needs, including food, housing, and medical care, and they rally against the system that created the injustice causing the crisis. The system is often used in marginalized communities where there is a need, especially Black communities, the working poor, LGBTQ+ communities, and migrant groups.

But don't call it charity. Mutual aid groups use the phrase "Solidarity, not charity." What, you may be wondering, is the difference? Well, it turns out to be pretty vast. There's no 503c status in mutual aid groups, and participants help those in need directly. There's no recurring donation that the professionals distribute according to their bylaws. The mutual aid model is simpler and asks fewer questions of those in need.

If someone requests aid from a nonprofit, there are often criteria that must be met. Sometimes the person in need must live in a certain zip code, or commit to sobriety, for example. Maybe the person's immigration status prohibits the nonprofit from helping. But in a mutual aid network, the criteria are more straightforward. You need help. That's it. No questions or expectations. You need help, and that is what mutual aid does.

In eastern Kentucky, a mutual aid group that formed at the beginning of the pandemic described itself as "just a bunch of hillbillies swapping hand-me-downs and filling up mason jars full of hand sanitizer." But more than a year later, the group has roughly three thousand members responding to requests or offering unsolicited help and information, such as available canned goods or job postings.

The requests are frequent. Someone needs ten dollars for gas so she can take her daughter to the doctor. A family is no longer able to afford its dogs, can anyone take them? As the temperature drops, there are many requests for kerosene to warm homes and make the chilly nights less so. Someone shares a quote from a book by Benjamin Jones with a photo of a tiny house surrounded by lush trees in a holler—"There's a part of Kentucky where they raise fast thoroughbreds on beautiful rolling horse farms, but I'm not from there. I'm from the hard-scrabble place where nothing ever came easy. I'm from the place where families used to scratch out a living on an old, rocky hillside farm, and men crawled into the belly of the mountain with a pickaxe to gouge out the coal. I'm from Eastern Kentucky. I'm from the hard part."

The social media page Appalachian Feminist Coalition amplifies mutual aid requests between funny memes and useful information. They have an online store with merch featuring Dolly Parton, bell hooks, and a design with daisies and morels with the phrase "Holler for Help,

Mutual Aid in the Mountains." The page bio describes itself as "the trailer park of intersectional feminism," which one fan admired as self-deprecating. But an AFC moderator quickly jumped in to clarify that isn't meant to be self-deprecating at all, it's an honor.

"I spent the majority of my young life living in trailer parks," said "Mod Ash" in a post. "Nobody ever goes without in a trailer park. Growing up, if my neighbors had it, so did I. If I was hungry, they fed me. If my single mother had something wrong with our car, they'd help fix it. Did heat go out? They'd bring us kerosene heaters, and vice versa. For me, it's a point of pride and nothing to be ashamed of."

Fighting for Food Justice through Racial Justice

In the commonwealth's largest city, Louisville, and its county, the income disparity is drastic, especially between the East End and West End of the city. The median household income in Jefferson County is more than $48,695—comfortably above the poverty line. But the median household income for residents of West Louisville is less than $22,000. For some areas within the West End, there is even deeper poverty. For example, in the Russell neighborhood the median income is only $9,000, which is not enough to cover twelve months of rent.

Shauntrice Martin was born in Louisville's West End and grew up in the Sheppard Square Housing Projects in the downtown Smoketown neighborhood. In her thirties she lived in Maryland and took part in a grocery co-op in a trendy art community right outside of Washington, D.C. That's where she saw bok choy for the first time.

For Martin, this new experience brought into focus her upbringing in a food desert where fresh food and produce were scarce. She claims a child in the West End is much more likely to be familiar with pizza rolls than plantains. She's concerned because public health issues in the West End are much more dire than elsewhere in the city. West End residents have a greater rate of infant mortality, diabetes, and heart disease, and an overall lower life expectancy.

More than 60,000 people live in West Louisville, but aside from the meager selections at convenience and liquor stores, the entire area really has only one grocery store, a Kroger. Although the West End may share a high rate of poverty with McCreary County in the southern part of the state, the two areas differ widely in the availability of food. In McCreary, there are nearly two hundred farms. Residents can get locally grown produce, fresh beef, eggs, and even art at the local farmer's market. The county also has a Kroger featuring a sprawling produce section with fruits and veggies piled high and organized by variety and color.

Oh, another difference between McCreary County and the West End of Louisville? About 98 percent of McCreary County residents are white, and about 80 percent of the residents of West Louisville are Black. Advocates like Martin believe food insecurity and race are so interconnected, the best way to promote food justice is through racial justice.

Martin knew the availability of fresh food in the West End was drastically different not only from the faraway co-op she once participated in, with its wide selection of organic produce and vegan options, but from areas close to home. Even the West End's sole grocery store was vastly different from the other Krogers throughout the city. To illustrate these differences, Martin organized a volunteer-led photo essay project called the Bok Choy Project documenting the current state of the various stores and especially the produce sections while answering the following questions:

- Did the store have any empty sections?
- Were there expired items?
- Was there a lack of organic options?
- Was bok choy available?

Volunteers also were asked to note store hours and anything notably different about the store compared to other Kroger stores in the area.

The first photo in the series is from a Kroger on Taylorsville Road serving a zip code that is about 11 percent Black. The store is open daily from 6 a.m. until midnight. The photos show a gorgeous produce section with fresh ginger, colorful peppers, radishes, parsnips, all under a constant mist of water. Also, they had lots of bok choy.

Other photos of other Kroger stores show similar selections and circumstances. One store may have been running a bit low on eggplant, so could present a problem if you were planning to invite the neighborhood over for eggplant parmigiana, but otherwise you could purchase any produce your heart desired. They may even have had enough eggplant for the neighborhood in the stockroom. For the most part, if you wanted a dragon fruit at 11 p.m., it wasn't a problem. Lots of fresh food, long hours of availability, and bok choy.

The West Broadway location serving a 92 percent Black population was in stark contrast, with the photos revealing empty shelves bearing only bright yellow price tags on the edge. The produce section was much smaller than other stores' and featured very common items—apples, bananas, pineapples, peppers, broccoli. The most exotic item I could spot was an individually wrapped package of kiwi. Definitely no bok choy.

Not only was the food selection drastically different, but the store hours were limited as well, opening at 7 a.m. and closing at 9 p.m. There was also a police officer stationed in front of the store in a cruiser. According to volunteer reports, the only other Kroger store with a police presence was in a zip code with a 59 percent Black population. (That store didn't have bok choy either.)

I contacted Kroger about these disparities. This was their response:

Over the past 10 years, we have invested $1.4 million into our Portland location ($1.2 million in the past 3 years) which the company built brand new in 2005. We have invested $4 million in our Broadway location ($920,000 in the past 3 years).

Kroger is committed to being in stock and offering fresh, healthy groceries to all customers. Our Portland and Broadway locations have incredible teams working hard every day to have the items our customers need in stock. If there is an item a customer would like to see in-store the produce teams have the ability to order the request if the product is available.

Kroger also runs the Zero Hunger, Zero Waste Mobile Market in partnership with Dare to Care food bank. This mobile grocery store serves the West End and provides fresh grocery produce for customers struggling to access traditional grocery stores.

To combat the persistent disparities, Martin formed the Feed the West movement, which strives to provide fresh, healthy food to residents of the West End. The movement was born out of urgent and immediate need. After the killing of Breonna Taylor by police, protests erupted across the city. During one night of protests, the National Guard patrolled through West Louisville and local barbecue restaurateur David McAtee was killed. After the killing, Kroger boarded up the windows of the West End store and announced it would be closed indefinitely.

Knowing that this store closing would leave many residents without access to food, Martin contacted her friend Taylor Ryan, founder of the nonprofit Change Today, Change Tomorrow, and asked what they could do together to help. They stayed awake until 2 or 3 a.m. making flyers, printing volunteer forms, and devising a plan to feed the community.

They awoke the next morning to hundreds of inquiries, including volunteers ready to bag and distribute groceries, as well as donations. Local partners provided distribution sites, and between the donations and the volunteer network, they quickly had the infrastructure necessary to meet the immediate need of providing food to West End residents. In the beginning of June alone, Feed the West served 7,000 people and provided more than half a million dollars in groceries.

Today Feed the West is thriving and has a brick-and-mortar storefront selling bundles of fresh food and featuring local, Black-owned small businesses. The Black Market's website features a "Black List" with a wide variety of goods, from homemade herbal teas to ice cream, as well as services such as meal prep and marketing. Black-owned farms which often provide produce to the market are also featured.

Finding Joy

Although Change Today, Change Tomorrow is practically in its infancy, the organization has been at the forefront of empowering the Black community and combatting poverty. The group works in conjunction with Feed the West to provide healthy food to residents in need. But there aren't stipulations or requirements for obtaining food or services. Right now you can access their website and fill out a request for food, noting any special requests such as baby formula or paper products, and a volunteer will deliver those goods to your door, no questions asked. As founder Taylor Ryan puts it, she's not just feeding poor people and qualifying each donation, she's just feeding people.

Amid poverty, there is joy. You just have to find it, seek it, hold on to it, and you have to build community around it.
—Taylor Ryan

I spoke to Ryan about the phenomenal impact CTCT has made in such a brief time. At only thirty, Ryan conceived the group during an assignment when she was earning her master's degree—her second master's degree—in Leadership Studies with an emphasis on non-profits and the public sector. That was in 2018. CTCT was then just a homework assignment, and now the organization has served more than 100,000 marginalized residents of Louisville. Within two years of its foundation, the organization was securing corporate donations from Louisville-based companies such as Humana and Churchill Downs to continue its work.

When I mention these things, Ryan frankly seems a bit unfazed as she entertains her toddler. Some local nonprofits put a lot of effort into fund-raising events such as glitzy galas and spend a lot of time talking about the work, a lot, before actually doing any type of work. At CTCT they just dive right in and do the work that they see needs to be done. Ryan is so focused on what's next and what is needed, she doesn't seem to have the time to pat herself on the back for what she's accomplished so far. She also may be *tired*. Not only is this mentally taxing and physically demanding work, but she is also personally doing as much of it as she can. If you request groceries, she's likely the one delivering. If you call the organization, you won't get her secretary, because there is no secretary. She's answering the phone.

The people that do work alongside her at CTCT or collaborate with her through their organizations are relentlessly working to help the community too. Remember when Martin and Ryan stayed up until the wee hours of the morning organizing an emergency supply of food because Kroger was unexpectedly closing? That's the kind of people powering CTCT. They literally cannot sleep knowing their neighbors may go hungry, and thanks to this benevolent ambition, they don't.

CTCT's mission is to eradicate the barriers plaguing the Black community—and the Black community is disproportionately affected by poverty in Louisville. Through the Umoka Project, volunteers go to the sea of tents where so many unhoused stay, and they deliver hot meals, snacks, and toiletries. They supply free period products weekly, filling a desperate need for an item that is rarely donated to other organizations serving the houseless. They host baby showers for expecting moms and provide them with diapers, onesies, and baby gear while celebrating. They provide free tutoring support for children learning virtually during the COVID-19 pandemic. They operate a storefront and help Black business owners gain exposure and promote their businesses.

Following the mutual aid model, their many endeavors feel more like solidarity than charity. They not only strive to provide the Black community with basic needs such as food, but they also treat people with dignity as they are being served. They empower the community with the tools they need to thrive, not just survive.

Although Ryan's work is defined as empowering the Black community, and the organization is so deeply involved in racial justice, when I ask about her childhood, she describes living in a trailer with her fifteen siblings in western Kentucky. As a biracial child and one of the oldest, she explains how she grew up in what she describes as a poor white family. She took care of her siblings and got her first job at thirteen. Today she's a highly educated executive director of a thriving organization. But she still considers herself poor. The organization is unlike other organizations in many ways, including not giving executives like Ryan six-figure salaries. Plus, while she has three degrees to show for her years of hard work, she also has nearly a quarter of a million dollars in student loan debt.

At CTCT, the gatekeeping aspect of accessing help is eliminated. There are many reasons someone may need immediate groceries and yet not meet official poverty guidelines. There's no income tax examination happening. It's disturbingly easy for working-class persons to suddenly find themselves unable to feed their families, especially in unprecedented times such as the pandemic. But Ryan doesn't care about the reasons behind the need, how significant or insignificant the need may be, she only cares about feeding people who say they need to be fed.

"There are people who are living in poverty, but they are happy, you know?" said Ryan. "And I'm not going to take that joy away from them by calling them poor."

When I asked Ryan to elaborate, she laughed and asked, "Say more about being poor and happy?" Ryan approaches poverty as a systemic issue, it's statistics and numbers. But people are people, they're not just statistics and numbers, and they shouldn't be treated as if they were.

When public assistance and charity serve the poor, there's often quite a bit of gatekeeping surrounding their needs and behavior. There's often criticism of what someone purchases at the grocery with an EBT card (formerly known as food stamps). People express the view that if a purchase is being made with an EBT card, they want to see a cart full of healthy food and shelf-stable items like beans, certainly not junk food like soda or chips, and certainly nothing lavish like steak. It seems only normal to have opinions about food that is not going home with you if there's public assistance involved. There are also often conditions for receiving aid. When Governor Matt Bevin was running for office, he suggested random drug tests be performed for recipients of public assistance.

The "welfare queen" myth tells us that those depending on public assistance to survive are, first of all, almost always Black women with many children and are somehow taking advantage of the benefits and living lives of luxury. This stereotype has persisted for decades, with many citing it as an example of the dangers of public assistance. But as the myth has persisted, it seems that an ideal welfare recipient has also emerged. With all this policing of what is and isn't appropriate in terms of assistance, if assistance *is* needed, it must be temporary. The recipient must abstain from drugs, alcohol, and Cheetos. The recipient who is without a job must be very actively looking for one.

And joy? Joy?!? Joy is not in the equation. I have never heard someone in a nonprofit describe the people in need as joyous. I've never associated being poor with being happy. When we continue to gatekeep poverty and determine who is worthy and who is not, while meeting only their most basic needs and nothing more, if there's anything I'd associate with poverty, it would be suffering. After all, when people are enraged by the "welfare queen" stereotype, isn't it the joy of a poor Black woman they find most offensive?

To call attention to the joy felt despite being poor seems like a truly radical statement, not only in the non-profit world but in our capitalist society.

"The world doesn't think poor people should be happy," said Ryan. "When you see us on trips, know that we went several days without eating to make that money happen. Maybe we sacrifice a bill a couple of months, and even if you see us getting the steak and shrimp in our baskets at Kroger, know that we're still swiping an EBT card.

"There are ways to be happy and still experience the aesthetics of this rich world. People are happy amid all this trauma. I picked up my boyfriend, who works at the Parkland Boys and Girls Club. There are shootings in Parkland almost every day. Not even a block away, I hear POP, POP, POP, POP! Kids are literally skipping. While seeing joy, you hear trauma. Even amid trauma, there is joy. Amid poverty, there is joy. You just have to find it, seek it, hold on to it, and you have to build community around it."

Empower the Poor

- Look at the big picture and, like Ben Carter, attack the systemic issues facing the poor. Follow the actions of the state and federal legislatures. On the Kentucky Equal Justice Center website, there is a fantastic database of introduced bills that affect the poor. Stay diligent and contact your representatives concerning these actions.
- Take care of your neighbors. Find those who need help through a mutual aid network like Eastern Kentucky Mutual Aid. If you have the means to support monetarily, you can either donate to a general fund that helps those in need or respond to requests directly. Even if you aren't in a position to help financially, you can look for other requests such as job leads, hand-me-downs, and more.
- Strive for food justice in your community, like Shauntrice Martin. Many have referred to areas like the West End of Louisville as a food desert. But food justice activists prefer the term "food apartheid," as it approaches the entire system and considers income, race, and geography. This is exactly how Feed the West approaches the issue. They not only ask why there

isn't bok choy in a produce section but why there is a police officer at the door. Ask these same questions, and help support the fight for food justice with your dollars, donations, and time.

- Find the joy, like Taylor Ryan. Approach the issue of poverty as a systemic, nuanced problem and treat people with compassion, empathy, and dignity. Encourage those in need not only to survive but to thrive.

TWO

ENVIRONMENT

HIS THICK New York accent serves as a dead giveaway that Craig Williams isn't from around these parts. Certainly not from the picturesque Berea, where he's made his home. At twenty, Williams studied Vietnamese at the Defense Language Institute in preparation for deployment during the Vietnam War. Shortly after, he served in Vietnam, speaking directly with the locals and translating for his fellow service members.

Many serve in the military and learn to conform to authority. Williams learned to question it.

When he returned to the States, he quickly found an activist home at Vietnam Veterans Against the War. He served on the steering committee of the organization that, as the name suggests, opposed policy and participation in the Vietnam War. The group also advocated for peace, justice, and the rights of American veterans who struggled to obtain treatment for post-traumatic stress disorder and recognition of toxic exposure from Agent Orange.

During his reintegration to civilian life, Williams found a community of like-minded peace- and earth-loving activists in California. One of them hailed from Kentucky and idyllically described the sprawling affordable land available—perfect for growing farms and families. So Williams decided to move and take root in Kentucky. He studied philosophy at Eastern Kentucky University, obtaining a bachelor's degree. After graduating, he worked in the public defender's office. Then he engaged in more creative pursuits, owned a woodworking business, and started a family.

In the mid-1980s, around the time Williams was firmly settled in his Kentucky home, the United States Congress mandated the destruction of the country's aging chemical weapons. For a peace-loving vet, the news that such lethal weapons would be destroyed and not used to destroy lives anywhere was good news. But the problem in eliminating chemical weapons was *how* they would be eliminated.

Many serve in the military and learn to conform to authority. Williams learned to question it.

Just several miles from his home, the Blue Grass Army Depot housed about five hundred tons of chemical weapons such as mustard gas and a VX nerve agent. As you may imagine, destroying tons and tons of chemical weapons is not easy. There are two common ways to approach the task. Incineration uses a very high temperature to eliminate the chemical weapons, which are then released as ash, water vapor, and carbon dioxide. Neutralization breaks down the chemical weapons using water and a compound such as sodium hydroxide.

Until the 1970s, the United States used some pretty questionable methods of destroying chemical weapons, and when I say "pretty questionable," the question is "My God, what were they thinking?" These methods included burying the weapons, burning them in open pits, and throwing them into the ocean. Such methods, as you may imagine, carried some rather disastrous long-term health and environmental consequences.

After World War II, believe it or not, burying chemical weapons was thought to be safe and generally seemed like a good idea. Chemical weapons were buried in mass quantities at the Redstone Arsenal near Huntsville, Alabama. Years after this haphazard disposal of the most hazardous materials, residents became concerned about the potential health consequences associated with living near a chemical weapon graveyard. Three residents with leukemia particularly suspected there was a connection. Today an investigation and cleanup effort are ongoing, but this is especially difficult as it is largely unknown where exactly the chemical weapons are buried. Turns out the same masterminds who conducted the burials didn't think to mark the locations. The project is expected to end in 2042.

Now, compared to the methods previously thought to be safe, such as literally just throwing the chemical weapons in the ocean, incineration seems like a good bet. So the United States has invested millions in the construction of incinerators. But according to Williams, when the chemical weapons are incinerated, hundreds of toxic compounds are released into the air, and from the beginning he has perceived this as a serious concern for public health and safety. He may have had in mind the sprawling hollows of the Bluegrass that brought him to the commonwealth, or maybe he was wanting to be a good neighbor and look out for other Kentuckians. But I suspect a driving factor was that "probably safe" wasn't safe enough for him when considering the well-being of his family.

At a hearing in the 1980s regarding the proposed incinerators, Williams vowed, "We refuse to put our lives, our homes, our economies, our children at risk and we will stop this incinerator."

The Centers for Disease Control and Prevention claim the destruction of chemical weapons is safe, regardless of whether they are incinerated or neutralized. There is little concrete evidence from federal agencies that chemical weapon incineration poses a serious threat to the community if the process runs smoothly . . . but things don't always run smoothly.

In Kentucky, chemical leaks have occurred, and vapors from mustard gas were detected. U.S. Army officials claimed there was no threat to the public during these leaks. Williams and a political ally in his environmental endeavors, Senator Mitch McConnell (yes, *that*

Mitch McConnell), cited these accidents as further need to dispose of the chemical weapons as safely as possible.

Environmental activists like Williams are not easily swayed by the claims of officials that incinerating the chemical weapons is perfectly safe, and given Williams's personal history and knowledge of the threats that environmental factors pose, it's not much of a surprise. In the United States there have been many instances of the public being told a chemical exposure is safe, only to learn decades later that it was not. Williams's distrust of authority first sparked as a young translator in Vietnam who came home and opposed the war.

One of his first encounters with a hazardous chemical happened during his military service. Agent Orange was a tactical herbicide widely used by U.S. troops in Vietnam. Soldiers were told not to worry, and authority figures insisted that the chemical was harmless. However, Vietnam veterans are found to have much higher rates of various types of cancer and skin, nerve, and respiratory disorders. Health hazards related to Agent Orange also included birth defects in children born after deployment. The Agent Orange Act, which gave Vietnam vets eligibility to receive compensation and treatment, wasn't enacted until the 1990s, and the battle to confirm the health effects of the chemical, and to determine who is eligible for relief, persisted for more than four decades.

Now in his seventies, Craig Williams suffers from symptoms related to Agent Orange, like many Vietnam veterans. When federal agencies claimed there weren't any health hazards related to incinerating chemical weapons near his family home, he was skeptical and chose to fight for a safer alternative. Williams's skepticism of the safety of chemical weapon incineration may well have been influenced by the cycle of officials claiming something was safe, and then later conceding it was quite dangerous. You know the old adage: Fool me once . . .

So Williams immediately took on the Pentagon to stop the plans to incinerate chemicals such as mustard gas in the air he, his family, and his neighbors breathe. He rejected the Department of Defense's plan to build the incinerator near his home without public input from the community it would affect most. He formed the grassroots group Kentucky Environmental Foundation and demanded the federal government pursue safe alternatives. Along with Williams, hundreds of concerned Kentuckians protested the proposed plan by marching in the streets chanting, "No more burning, no more lies. Better way, neutralize!"

The environmental activists said neutralization would be safer for the environment and for the workers involved. When the chemical weapons are neutralized, nothing is released into the air. The process also is more controlled, allowing multiple treatments if necessary.

The grassroots activists fought against the incineration plans for a decade before Congress finally agreed to delay incineration while considering safer methods. But they still had the Pentagon to take on, which Williams described as "no easy task." The army recommended that incineration proceed. Despite KEF being severely outspent and outrepresented, they fought on and presented evidence that incineration was hazardous. From their perspective, if a safer alternative exists, why not do that?

Battling the Pentagon and the bureaucratic powers striving to build the incinerators lasted many years, with many whistles being blown, many testimonies given, many lawsuits filed, but eventually the little grassroots Kentucky group was successful in convincing several sites across the country to forgo incineration in favor of the alternative neutralizing methods.

Craig Williams served as an advisor at the Blue Grass Chemical Agent Disposal Plant (BGCAPP) during its construction, ensuring the safety of the plant's workers and the community. Today neutralization of the chemical weapons is under way at the BGCAPP. There are even videos on the Program Executive Office Assembled Chemical Weapons Alternatives pages on the United States Army website. The videos, set to upbeat background music, show employees working away in the plant and diagrams of the complicated process. They're reminiscent of episodes of *Mister Rogers' Neighborhood* that I remember watching as a small child, but instead of employees printing newspapers or wrapping mass-produced cookies, they're destroying chemical weapons.

The plant is a technologically advanced facility with huge robotic equipment performing various tasks. Workers in closest contact with the chemicals wear extremely complex hazmat suits to protect themselves as the most dangerous chemicals on the planet are neutralized after being stored nearby for decades. As of 2021, 98.9 tons have been destroyed.

By the way, that still leaves a good 424 tons to destroy in Kentucky, and the Kentucky stockpile represents a mere 2 percent of the chemical weapons in the United States. This gigantic stockpile of chemical weapons was never used, we just hoarded them for decades like a sentimental piece of old furniture that sits in the corner of your basement. The process of eliminating them takes decades and billions of dollars.

Now with the victory of defeating incineration behind them, KEF is focused on the de-militarized future in Kentucky. Currently, more than a thousand employees work at the disposal plant, and that number is projected to drop to zero after all the work is done in several years. Williams and KEF have been working with longtime political ally McConnell and others to avoid serious economic fallback from the closure and to stabilize the area's future economy. The neutralization process has brought many talented, highly educated workers to the area, and recognizing their contribution to the commonwealth, many are working hard to keep them here after the work is done.

Today Williams and other environmentally minded Kentuckians breathe a little easier knowing the world's most lethal weapons are being euthanized without doing harm to anyone.

Rubbertown Stinks

Much like the intersection of poverty and racial justice, it's impossible to critically examine environmental issues such as the rise of Rubbertown without also considering racial inequity.

When you enter the West Louisville neighborhood of Rubbertown, you may immediately notice . . . well, it smells. If you're not accustomed to the odor and haven't been "nose-blind" to it, as the air-freshener commercials warned us was a thing, you would likely become aware of the strange, unsettling odor in the air. It reminds me of something I might order from Amazon, arriving from overseas in a vacuum seal, which reviewers recommend "airing out" to let the chemical odor dissipate before using.

I first noticed it when I was writing an article for a local alt-weekly about community gardens, many of which were in impoverished neighborhoods such as Rubbertown. I remember standing beside a thriving vegetable garden as children tended the rows of tomatoes and peppers. But my eyes were focused on the sky as if my other senses might reveal the cause of the odor in the air. The adults were discussing the importance of growing fresh food and the influence on lifelong healthy eating habits, and all I wanted to ask was "Hey, y'all smell that too? Is that normal?"

The industrial complex off the Ohio River between the Chickasaw and Lake Dreamland neighborhoods in the West End of Louisville got its name from a large rubber manufacturer originally operated by the federal government, which now produces synthetic rubber used in tires. During World War II the area was booming, becoming home to several other companies, including oil refineries and a railroad tie manufacturer.

When Rubbertown first became a hotbed of industrial activity, the United States feared that the Japanese would cease the export of necessary supplies to the largest rubber-producing countries. So to prevent any serious production interruption to the rubber needed for the war effort, the United States government chose a city to produce synthetic rubber. Louisville won the lottery, or drew the short straw, depending on who you ask.

This boom of industrial activity naturally attracted workers to the area, and they went on to build homes nearby. Important note—they were white.

Later in the book I'm going to discuss Kentucky racial inequity in more detail, including housing discrimination and the chutzpah of one Kentucky couple who took a stand against the discriminatory housing system, which essentially barred Black people from owning property in certain areas. But for now, let's just dip our toes into the dirty waters of racist housing practices because it is necessary to understand Rubbertown.

In the early 1900s, segregation in housing was no accident, it was by design. The Roosevelt administration in the 1930s mapped cities and color-coded neighborhoods based on certain risk factors, such as the likelihood of foreclosure. These "risky" neighborhoods were color-coded red, and the practice—which, keep in mind, was largely designed by the federal government—is now known as "redlining." This practice is often referenced when discussing systemic racial issues in certain areas because redlining is such an important part of their history. Big surprise, the neighborhoods marked red had mostly Black residents.

In Louisville, the West End beyond 9th Street was mostly in the red. Not only was being labeled risky a huge burden for a potential homeowner trying to get a mortgage, but builders viewed it as too much of a liability as well. These barriers were especially difficult for first-time home buyers, because if you wanted to take advantage of a federal loan program such as the Federal Housing Administration (FHA) insured loan—still a popular option for first-time homeowners—the loan would carry some really expensive terms if you were looking to purchase a home in a redlined area.

The legend for urban real estate maps would grade areas by desirability. Those color-coded green were the best of the best, in demand whether times were good or bad. The second grade was color-coded blue, with homes that were "still desirable" and were expected to stay stable for at least several years but had probably reached their peak. The third grade was color-coded yellow, appropriately looking like caution lights throughout the edges of the city signifying a "definite decline" and the not so subtle "infiltration by a lower grade population." The fourth and lowest grade was color-coded red. Stop. Do not pass. These red-coded areas were bleakly described: "the only hope is for the demolition of these buildings and transition of this area into a business district" as well as "this particular spot is a blight on the surrounding areas."

On a map from the 1930s, although some nearby areas had spots of blue and yellow meant to signify some economic potential and promise, the Rubbertown area was red.

White homeowners were the inaugural residents of the Rubbertown area, benefiting from the nearby jobs. But after World War II, homeowners weren't seeing the value of their homes increase. For members of the working class, the purchase of a house is likely the biggest investment they'll ever make. If the investment doesn't pay off, that's extremely worrisome.

Then the environmental impact of living near a booming industrial complex began to show in the form of wind and soot, not exactly homey. The coal smoke in the air was a visible problem.

So between the investment in their homes declining after the area was redlined and the unsettling environmental side-effects of capitalism at work in their backyard, the homeowners began moving to areas of the city "green-lit" for prosperity, such as Mockingbird Valley and Indian Hills, where the home values were high and the people happened to be white.

The government didn't have a legal obligation to address the troubling environmental issues, so guess what? They just didn't.

The city sought to address this problem by forming the Louisville Smoke Commission and then passed a smoke ordinance. Its effectiveness was fairly limited, as it extended only to the city limits and did not apply to private residences. Eventually, though, the state legislature passed a bill allowing the Smoke Commission to regulate pollution beyond the city limits, including Rubbertown.

To illustrate how serious (and disgusting) the problem was during the 1950s, the method of measuring air pollution was to hang buckets on lampposts throughout Jefferson County and collect soot. How bad was the pollution? Buckets and buckets would show you.

Around this time of coal ash hanging in the air and white flight in full effect, Black families began moving to areas of West Louisville including Rubbertown. Hunter S. Thompson wrote about the white flight phenomenon in his book *The Great Shark Hunt: Strange Tales from a Strange Time.* Homeowners, citing concerns about their home values, were selling as quickly as they could, with some blocks having as many as ten "for sale" signs in their yards. Thompson quoted one urban renewal official regarding the movement of Black residents into the West End: "Sure they move to the West End. Where else can they go?"

In 1956, after the Kentucky legislature gave the Louisville Smoke Commission more power to evaluate how severe a problem the pollution was, a new Air Pollution Control Board (APCB) was formed. The APCB used resources from city, county, state, and federal agencies and conducted a study for two years. The study revealed sky-high amounts of carcinogens in the air around Rubbertown. Unfortunately, the issue of potential health hazards persisted for decades without a significant resolution. Maybe if there was a high level of carcinogens in the air around Indian Hills, the issue would have been addressed, but there was a stalemate in Rubbertown.

After World War II, private companies had taken up residence in Rubbertown, and it remained a thriving production hub with lots of business and lots of air pollution. The businesses had no interest in leaving. Many residents not only were interested in leaving but were desperate to do so. But leaving would require them to sell their homes for a fair price and find new places to live that were comparable in price, which was a virtual impossibility. As the official told Thompson in the 1960s, "Where else could they go?"

The health consequences of living in Rubbertown are not easily pinned down. Many residents have stories of living through chemical leaks, spills, and even explosions at a nearby plant and also stories of experiencing kidney stones, cancer, Crohn's disease, and daily struggles such as trouble sleeping due to odors and respiratory distress. But proving that those health issues are due to the emissions is extremely difficult. It takes years to conduct studies, form commissions, pass regulations. In the meantime, people are living in the neighborhood and breathing that air every day.

Erica Peterson, an environmental reporter with WFPL aimed to answer the question of whether residents of Rubbertown had a higher chance of developing cancer than the average person. Anecdotal evidence pointed that way.

Indeed, rates of lung cancer turned out to be almost 35 percent higher in Rubbertown than in other neighborhoods of the city. Similarly, rates of colorectal cancer were 31 percent higher. Kentucky's Department for Public Health also examined cancer rates in Rubbertown, but although the rates were higher than expected, they weren't high enough to determine a definite link. Even with the significant jumps in lung and colorectal cancer rates, a link cannot be determined, because there are too many other potential factors at play.

In lung cancer, for instance, smoking is the top culprit, but environmental factors are potential causes as well. Say a smoking resident of Rubbertown is diagnosed with lung cancer. Was the lung cancer caused by smoking or by radon exposure? Can't say. In her work, Peterson consulted Dr. Tom Tucker, the head of the Kentucky Cancer Registry. Tucker explained that while many non-environmental risk factors play a role in developing lung cancer, environmental factors can't be ruled out. It's just not possible to determine a causal link between lung cancer and the environment of Rubbertown with the data available.

Another of the apparent factors determining health risks is income level. Rubbertown is one of the poorest neighborhoods in the city, and poor people generally suffer more health problems, for reasons that include lack of access to healthcare and to healthy, fresh food.

What we do know is that the residents disproportionately report either personally having cancer or knowing a fellow resident or family member with cancer. We also know that Jefferson County had the highest level of air toxins according to an EPA study from 2002, and 42 percent of the air emissions in the entire county are from Rubbertown. We know that according to the findings of the Air Pollution Control District, the cancer risk is more than three times the maximum acceptable rate set by the EPA. Granted, it cannot be determined without a shadow of a doubt that living in Rubbertown leads to increased health hazards, but there has certainly been enough problematic empirical evidence, along with tons of anecdotal evidence when we listen to the people who live there, to at the very least consider it a strong possibility.

With the firm belief that protest is the most effective tool to enact positive change, Reverend Louis Coleman fought injustice armed only with a bullhorn for decades. He founded the Justice Resource Center, fighting injustice and discriminatory practices throughout Kentucky. He learned about segregation through his lived experience of growing up in the heavily segregated neighborhood of Smoketown in Louisville. His faith pushed him toward the constant pursuit of social justice. The industrial emissions that residents worried were causing their many health problems brought Coleman to Rubbertown.

Reverend Coleman was not specifically an environmental activist, he was a fighter of injustice, and what he heard from the residents of Rubbertown—the complaints of toxic air causing asthma, cancer, and other ailments, complaints that went unheard—was injustice worth fighting. He formed a grassroots organization, the Rubbertown Emergency ACTion (REACT), with other local activists who were like-minded in their commitment to pursuing clean air through peaceful protest.

The group recruited residents by leaving flyers at doors with information about upcoming direct actions and meetings. They attended city council meetings and protested pending permits for industry while continuing to mobilize the community and push people to take action against such a chronic problem. Before the formation of REACT, concerns had been raised for decades, with some alarming data, but the calls to action were mostly going unheard. This group demanded to be heard.

If any local government official or representative of industry was going to speak on the issue of air quality or any issue facing Rubbertown, REACT was going to make sure they were a part of that conversation and their voices would be heard. The volume of Reverend Coleman's bullhorn garnered the attention of local media, and the group gained publicity for their efforts and, most important, attention to the air quality affecting their lives.

In response to REACT's publicity, Louisville mayor Jerry Abramson met with companies operating in Rubbertown concerning air quality, and tangible results finally began. One large corporation, American Synthetic Rubber Company, installed pollution controls that drastically reduced emissions. The company is still in operation, so I suppose reducing carcinogens wasn't too harmful to their bottom line. Opponents of the plan warned that jobs would be lost if the plan was put in place, but it seems that jobs were not lost to any environmental regulations.

After more than a decade of protests, demands, and negotiations, Louisville's Strategic Toxic Air Reduction (STAR) program was launched. The STAR program fought toxic air with accountability and it set rules that toxic polluters had to abide by. Not only was the program effective, it has even been singled out as a model by federal agencies such as the EPA. Finally it was no longer a case of "If you want to see toxic air, look at Louisville," but "If you want to see how to fight toxic air, look at Louisville."

As a result of the STAR program, toxic air emissions decreased by 73 percent between 2005 and 2017. One specific carcinogen, 1,3-butadiene, presents as a colorless gas and has an odor that also may remind you of gas. It's mostly used to produce rubber, and exposure to it, including in the air near a facility producing it, can cause leukemia. After the enforcement of the STAR program, emissions of 1,3-butadiene have fallen more than 75 percent.

Reverend Coleman died in 2008 before the most substantial effects of his activism could be realized. Currently, Rubbertown remains home to eleven industrial plants, and although emissions along with the hazards they carry have been drastically reduced, there are still emissions and potential health hazards concerning the residents of Rubbertown.

REACT is still active, notifying members and residents of upcoming meetings and warning of any dangerous emissions in the air occurring from an unexpected leak, for example. Permits are still protested. Accountability sessions are still proposed. And, well, as I mentioned earlier, Rubbertown still kind of stinks.

If Reverend Coleman and his bullhorn were still out in the city, they'd likely still have work to do alongside a new group of REACT activists in Rubbertown.

Fight for Your Environment

- Don't fear a fight too big. Look at the example Craig Williams set in his fight against the Pentagon. If he can take on the military-industrial complex in the fight for cleaner air, surely your fight seems more manageable.
- Demand to be heard like Reverend Coleman. Use the tools and resources available to ensure your message reaches the right people. Sometimes you don't need deep pockets or connections to the right people, you just need a loud enough bullhorn.

- Listen and amplify the unheard voices in your community. The grassroots activists of REACT proved to be so effective because they were determined, focused, organized, and relentless in their fight. Keep your own goals in mind, and learn from their example of what is possible.

THREE

RELIGION

AFTER THE GRAND JURY declined to charge the officers involved in the killing of Breonna Taylor, at least in any way that looked like justice to the many protestors who had been occupying the downtown streets of Louisville, protestors continued to chant her name and demand an end to police brutality, carrying signs and bullhorns as they marched.

Before the decision was announced on September 23, 2020, Louisville city officials appeared to prepare for war. The courthouse near Jefferson Square Park—reclaimed as "Injustice Park" by protestors—had large sheets of plywood covering the windows. Businesses all around the downtown area were likewise boarded up to protect from vandalism. Streets where protestors had consistently demonstrated were closed with concrete blockades that couldn't be moved without heavy machinery.

The National Guard was called in, and armed members stood beside armored vehicles in intersections and areas generally known for tourist activity, such as Fourth Street Live. Mayor Greg Fischer announced a curfew, which would apply unless you were commuting for work, seeking medical attention for yourself or others, or going to a house of worship. After 9 p.m. anyone out for any other reason—e.g., protesting—would be subject to arrest.

Throughout the protests, police had responded to crowds demonstrating in the street by deploying tear gas, rubber bullets, and stun grenades, also known as flashbangs, which create a loud noise and bright light meant to disorient people. In the crowd-control crossfire, a local news reporter was even pelted with pepper balls on live TV by a police officer despite her fluorescent vest identifying her as a member of the media.

Months earlier, the National Guard had been called in to enforce a previous curfew. Although protests had mostly been focused downtown, Guard members were roaming the West End on the night of June 1. Many people were gathering outside a convenience store and barbecue restaurant. According to witnesses in the area, that was just Sunday night. People gathered weekly to socialize on late summer nights while smoke and the smell of pork ribs billowed out of Yaya's grills. David "Yaya" McAtee was well known in the West End not only for his delicious barbecue but for his hospitality. He had many regular customers and had friendly relationships with the local police officers, often serving them on the house. Nights like this, the people gathering for barbecue looked less like a crowd in a restaurant full of strangers and more like a bunch of friends having a party.

Those on the scene that night claimed that as police and Guard members roamed the streets enforcing the curfew, they herded people into a small area. This tactic is known as kettling, as police move to control a crowd in a limited space, which then forces the crowd to either take an exit controlled by the police or remain contained and be arrested.

In this case, the kettling maneuver sent the crowd to Yaya's small restaurant and outdoor space. This caused mass confusion as people began running in response to seeing others run. (After all, if someone looks terrified and runs in one direction, you probably also run instead of investigating the cause.) Pepper balls were suddenly fired into the crowd, hitting drinks and a doorway and just narrowly missing McAtee's niece's head. Panic set in. In such a chaotic moment, it likely wasn't clear that the projectiles were the generally nonlethal pepper balls and not live gunfire.

After his niece entered the kitchen describing her close call, McAtee walked to the door to investigate with his hand placed on the pistol holstered at his right side. He took a step out of the doorway, raised his arm in the air as someone firing a warning shot would, and fired his pistol. Nineteen shots were then fired in his direction, with two resulting in his death.

Those moments—protestors personally witnessing police brutality, experiencing the gasping for air after tear gas fills it, singing "Amazing Grace" outside Yaya's restaurant once his body was finally removed after lying at the scene for more than twelve hours—were fresh in the minds of protestors as this new curfew was enforced. Since the last curfew enforcement with National Guard support had ended someone's life, the tension was palpable.

The only Black woman in the Kentucky state legislature, Representative Attica Scott, was protesting alongside her constituents and her teenage daughter, Ashanti, that evening. The mother and daughter had protested for many days downtown, despite one day being hit without warning with a cloud of tear gas.

Before the curfew, Attica Scott and Ashanti were among twenty-two protestors arrested and were accused of first-degree rioting, unlawful assembly, and failure to disperse. The charges were dropped, but if Representative Scott had been convicted of rioting, a class D felony, the author of Breonna's Law banning no-knock warrants like the one involved in Breonna Taylor's death would have been ineligible to vote according to Kentucky law.

Scott was quick to point out to me that a class D felony was the same class as the charge on which the grand jury indicted Louisville Metro Police officer Brett Hankison in connection with Breonna Taylor's death. She said she spent ten hours in jail, while Hankison spent thirty minutes.

Local and state government, police, and the Guard had the resources and the numbers to respond to any potential insurrection. When a business was vandalized as well as a few city buses, police quickly reported. Then the harshest act of vandalism occurred when a window of the downtown public library was broken and a flare was thrown inside. After Attica Scott, a strong supporter of the public libraries and advocate for the library workers' union, was arrested, she was told of the library vandalism and of the suspicion that she could have been involved.

"Stop feeling like because someone carries a gun and is in uniform that they're telling the truth," said Representative Scott, shaking her head. "If I had not been going live on Instagram at the moment that we were arrested, people would have believed them! They would have believed we tried to firebomb the library. I'm like the biggest nerd around! In what world, what part of the United States, do you see people [who are] fighting for the movement for Black lives burning libraries?!

"To have my daughter with me and know that there's nothing I can do to keep her safe, when you know one of the officers spent thirty minutes in jail and we spent ten hours? It's unbelievable. It's absolutely unbelievable."

By 9 p.m. the curfew was officially in effect and the familiar warning came from the loudspeakers: "*This is an unlawful assembly . . .*" Police in riot gear marched forward toward the crowd, forcing protestors to choose either vacating the area or marching toward the line of shields and helmets. The crowd dispersed, but most of the protestors remained in the same general vicinity. More groups of police approached from the other direction, and the protestors were a bit stuck as police used the familiar kettling tactic used on the night of McAtee's death.

Then the doors of First Unitarian Church opened, and members of the congregation and clergy came out and instructed protestors, "This is a house of worship. We are exempt from the emergency order. You're safe here."

Church members quickly transformed their sanctuary into a sanctuary for protestors dodging arrest. Unitarians are known to be politically progressive, and quite a few of the congregants had recollections of fighting for marriage equality, for women's rights, and for an end to the war in Vietnam. But many of the mostly white congregation reflected that they did not have personal experience fighting for racial justice.

In this self-reflection, they recognized the moments in history when they could proudly recall they had fought the good fight. But they also recalled the times they didn't show up and didn't recognize the struggles so many others faced. Antiracism is a constant practice, it's not a course you can take or a book that you can read that will give you all the knowledge you'll ever need. It's an ongoing introspective journey. Many congregants had individually embraced this antiracist journey, and when opportunities to right the wrongs of their past arose, they took them.

They hung a Black Lives Matter sign on the front of the old church, illuminated between stained glass windows. But as I've been told by local Black activists, there can be a performative element to social justice. Change Today, Change Tomorrow founder Taylor Ryan described entering stores that displayed Black Lives Matter signs in their front windows, only to notice the familiar motion of the people inside clutching their purses. How can the statement feel genuine when Black people don't feel like they matter when they enter?

To show that Black lives matter, the church needed to demonstrate their convictions with their actions, and they had ample opportunity. The church is located a short walk from the square where protestors had been gathering. To support the ongoing demonstration, congregants collected water and first aid supplies and often made deliveries to distribute these. Volunteers saw the wounds caused by police control measures, such as injuries from tear gas canisters or pepper balls. One congregant even experienced being tear-gassed directly while delivering aid.

When a bunch of protestors suddenly found themselves trapped by police and needing aid, the church took that opportunity too. Soon both the inside and outside of the church were filled with people. The church members used the first aid supplies they had on hand to attend to anyone wounded. In classic church fashion, they offered "refreshments." They ransacked the cabinets to gather enough food to feed anyone hungry. They even had legal aid available. In their minds, wasn't this the righteous thing to do, heal the wounded, shelter those in need of sanctuary, and feed the hungry?

For hours the church served as a safe place as police in riot gear and clutching batons remained outside, recognizing the loophole that prohibited them from entering a house of worship. Eventually they allowed protestors to exit the church grounds, return to their cars or otherwise catch rides home, and gather their belongings left at the square without being arrested.

The church continued to offer sanctuary as long as the curfew remained in effect. The congregants improved their skill at cooking pounds of macaroni and cheese and were able to meet the suddenly increased need through the generosity of others.

One congregant recalled a sermon delivered by Reverend Lori Kyle that described a bit of the backlash the church had received in response to its recent activities. An angry email said the sender had looked at the church's website and found no evidence of God. Reverend Kyle said she had seen God in all of their actions. When they gave a bottle of water to someone, God was there. When they offered comfort, God was there. When they applied a Band-Aid to someone, talked to someone recently released from jail, fed them, let them sleep, that's where the minister felt God's presence.

When I discuss the work that many activists and other change agents do, even if I don't bring up spirituality or religious belief, it comes up frequently. When I spoke to Ben Carter about the work he's doing with the Kentucky Equal Justice Center to help people avoid eviction along with other ways to help low-income Kentuckians in need, he personally was disheartened by the rush to "get back to normal" during the COVID-19 pandemic when financial crises had been the norm for so many, and he felt we had lost an opportunity to show true compassion toward our neighbors.

"It's sad to me, because I feel like there was a small window of time where we could have said, as a community and a nation, we're going to take better care of each other," said Carter. "And that just slammed shut. Think about what kind of spiritual transformation might have been possible as a society.

"I'm sure it's not convenient for most people that there's an airborne illness, you know, all around us. But nothing—nothing—can communicate our interconnectedness and our shared destiny in a way that a pandemic can, because all of a sudden, whether another person has access to healthcare or not, or the ability to make a good decision about whether to stay home from work that day or not—because they know they're going to be evicted if they don't go to work that week and they won't lose their job for making a responsible decision based on how they're feeling that day—they can get unemployment benefits all of a sudden!

"Like, that person making good decisions and having the ability to stay home, stay healthy away from me right now, impacts my destiny in a way that is just so visible and understandable. We really could have had this spiritual transformation that I think is necessary for more Kentuckians and for Americans to insist on the kind of policies that guarantee housing, healthcare, and food for all Americans."

Carter doesn't work for a religious organization, he's an attorney, and fighting for equity in justice for low-income Kentuckians doesn't necessarily sound like a spiritual battle. But his citing of religious beliefs reveals a bit about the personal motivations that brought him to the law and the work he does today. He values the idea of neighborliness and compassion toward others, according to him, because he's a Christian.

When I met first Pam McMichael to speak about her work with the Poor People's Campaign, if I didn't know and someone asked me to guess what occupation she held, I would have guessed minister, or at least what a minister is meant to be. Her presence is warm, and she's very soft-spoken but eloquent and thoughtful in her responses. She even naturally let out a couple of quiet bless-yous.

Changing the moral narrative is like the saying, what if the lion always tells the story, and you never know about the lamb?
—Pam McMichael

"I call myself a recovering Southern Baptist," said McMichael. "What draws me to this is the social justice, and I just feel like we're in the current time that the right-wing discriminatory, oppressive narrative has had too much public support, and faith leaders really have a critical role to play in . . . I don't say getting our country back, because we never really had it, but getting our country moving in more fair and just ways.

"Changing the moral narrative is like the saying, what if the lion always tells the story, and you never know about the lamb?"

Choosing Your Fight and Never Stopping Fighting

I was eager to meet Ira Grupper after he contacted our small, progressive Jewish organization. At the time, there were only four of us organizers receiving training and resources from the national organization. In my early thirties, I was the oldest and least hip.

Then I met Ira, who claimed he first became an activist in utero and thus had been an activist for seventy-seven years. He humbly referred to himself as a bit of a badass. And you know what? He *is*. This guy wearing suspenders, thick glasses, and what appear to be ortho-pedic sneakers is a complete badass.

Grupper was born in Brooklyn, New York, to an Orthodox Jewish family—holy rollers, he called them. He said his father was politicized during the Great Depression, but he "wasn't a heavy-duty activist like us." (Which completely flattered me.)

"I went to regular elementary school and cheder [Hebrew school] after," said Grupper. "This accomplished two things. One, I was bar mitzvahed. Two, I said I'll never set foot in another fucking synagogue."

In 1960 his father explained to sixteen-year-old Ira that he was going to support a sit-in at the neighborhood Wool-worth's lunch counter and join the picket line. After the historic sit-in in Greensboro, North Carolina, waves of sim-ilar demonstrations protesting their segregation policies had broken out at other Woolworth locations, including many in New York City. Grupper proudly recalled that most of the would-be patrons were working-class Jews from the neighborhood and very few crossed the picket line.

Like many working-class families in Brooklyn, Grup-per lived in a housing project owned by real-estate mogul Fred Trump and participated in rent strikes and the fight for housing justice, demanding livable conditions at sustainable prices.

As he deepened his commitment to racial equity, he knew he had to go to the place he called "the fulcrum of struggle," the Deep South. He worked for the Student Nonviolent Coordinating Committee in Atlanta alongside civil rights icons like John Lewis, Julian Bond, Stokely Carmichael, and Fannie Lou Hamer.

Civil rights activist Johnnie Mae Walker told Grupper he was "pretty smart for a white boy" and urged him to come to Hattiesburg to join the Mississippi Freedom Democratic Party. So he did.

During the summer of 1965, Grupper along with hundreds of other activists protested discriminatory action by the state legislature in Jackson, Mississippi. The state legislature was pushing forward segregation laws, even though they contravened the Civil Rights Act of 1964 and were patently unconstitutional. Grupper let me know he now had a severe case of CRS, otherwise known as "can't remember shit" disease, and as if to prove it, he told me this joke a second time during our conversation. However, when he told me about the protests and their aftermath in Mississippi, he remembered great detail, including the exact design of the billy clubs police used to beat the protestors and how they must have had a weight at the end.

The first group of protestors were arrested individually for distributing flyers. The flyers read:

CITIZENS OF JACKSON, WAKE UP! JOIN IN THE PROTEST. Police brutality in our city must go. Your voice against this evil must be heard. How long? How long? Must negros suffer the indignities heaped upon them? Several months ago, an 18-year-old was slain in the county jail by five officers of the law. To date, no action has been taken to bring the murderers to justice.

. . . We are conscious that a democratic government must be of the people, by the people, and for the people. We challenge the validity of those who hold elected offices who were not elected by the people and when elected enact laws which are designed to discriminate against one segment of the people.

Protestors were arrested in large groups: 200 for demonstrating without a permit, 75 for marching to the Capitol, 100 more in five separate demonstrations. According to

Grupper, a total of 950 were arrested, making it one of the largest mass arrests in the civil rights era. In the southern Black community he says he was privileged to live in, he attended church services with fellow activists and noticed the congregants calling each other "sister" and "brother." When he recalls demonstrating with a large group of other activists, he also refers to them as his sisters and brothers.

Many of his brothers and sisters in the movement were beaten by the police, one woman so badly that she suffered a miscarriage. In the movement, they all worked closely together and formed bonds much like a family. They cared for one another and did their best to protect each other. But when they were jailed, they were all separated. Women and men. White and Black.

Due to the overcrowding of the local jails and the large number of protestors arrested, hundreds of civil rights activists were imprisoned at the fairgrounds. The cattle were cleared out and the protestors were brought in. The conditions were so horrific, clergy representatives from the National Council of Churches of Christ testified before Congress after inspecting the makeshift jail and referred to it as a concentration camp. Reverend Ian McCrae, Reverend W. Raymond Berry, and John M. Pratt testified:

In Jackson, Mississippi, we saw—with our own eyes—fellow countrymen who were forced to remain all day on an absolutely bare concrete floor—denied even the opportunity to stretch out for a moment's rest on mattresses laid out only a few feet away.

We saw—with our own eyes—stitches in scalps, which closed the gashes inflicted by the clubs of policemen.

We talked with those prisoners and learned that no fresh fruit, no fresh milk, and no meat except for one bologna sandwich per prisoner on one day had been served within that compound since the first persons were interned in it seven days ago.

We are completely convinced that the Jackson concentration camp is not to serve as a place of incarceration, but rather to serve as a place to break the spirit, the will, the health, and even the body of each individual who dared to assemble peaceably to seek a redress of grievances.

In an address prepared for the New Jewish Agenda conference in 1991, Grupper recalled the experience, which he described to me as a profoundly religious one:

We arrived in prison trucks at the state fairgrounds, where cattle had been kept and then moved, and which were the same buildings where we would be housed. Women and men were separated, and I didn't see my jailed sisters in the struggle until we were released on bond about two weeks later.

After being booked, we had to pass through a cordon of Mississippi State Police. Some of us were beaten. In the cavernous hall where we wound up, there were additional beatings for protesting the cops segregating us—Black civil rights protestors on one side facing whites on the other.

When 'dinner' was to be served, the guards, as a form of control and humiliation, forced the whites to line up first. Each white inmate was given a slice of bologna stuck between two stale pieces of bread, and a paper cup with milk—or rather, tepid water with a little milk powder.

Each white guy returned with his meal to his spot on the cement floor on the 'white' side, sat down cross-legged, and placed the cup on the floor, sandwich on top of the cup, in front of him.

Then the brothers, the African-American civil rights prisoners, lined up to get their sandwich and milk. They returned to their spots on the 'colored' side, sat down cross-legged, placing their cups on the hard, cement floor, and sandwich on top.

There was no talking. No one ate. No one drank. After the last Black prisoner took his seat, all of us prisoners, Black and white together, and without pre-arrangement, picked up our sandwiches and broke bread as one.

As he told this story, which he's told many, many times over the past few decades, he suddenly got choked up reminiscing. He quickly wiped away a few tears. "If I were a Catholic, I would have thought of the Holy Communion. It was that kind of solidarity that made such an impact. I can't remember what I had for breakfast this morning, but I still remember that thing."

Sometime during his work in the South, he doesn't remember exactly when, he met Carl and Anne Braden. The Bradens convinced him to move to Louisville and work the printing press for their monthly newspaper, the *Southern Patriot*. Kentucky has been his home since.

In the early 1970s he had a hard time finding work because of his eyesight. He described himself as totally blind without correction. To work most factory jobs that he was qualified for, he would have to pass a physical, which he could not do. So he got creative.

"I would go sneak into the medical office and I would memorize the chart," he said. "Or I would ask someone similar to take the test for me. If I couldn't do that, I would pay somebody off."

Frustrated that he couldn't get a job as he normally would, due to circumstances beyond his control, he began researching his options. He spent time in the University of Louisville Law Library and finally found a loophole that would allow him to qualify for a job with his disability. If a company did business with the federal government, then they could not discriminate against someone with a disability. There must be reasonable accommodations.

Desperate for work to provide for his family and without the funds for legal counsel, he found some attorneys willing to work pro bono. He mentioned it was at a "very fancy, bourgeois firm downtown," where he showed up in jeans. Then a local council for the blind got involved. Soon enough he had twenty organizations and several attorneys taking his case.

The case was one of the first wins in the United States for disabled employees under the Rehabilitation Act of

1973 and served as a predecessor to the Americans with Disabilities Act. After winning the case, he finally got the job he fought so hard for and worked the assembly line at Philip Morris for twenty-four years. Although he's never smoked a cigarette, he now suffers from chronic obstructive pulmonary disease (COPD) from so much exposure to cigarette manufacturing.

Grupper has belonged for decades to the Kentucky Alliance Against Racist and Political Repression. The antiracist organization was formed some forty years ago by Anne Braden, Angela Davis, Suzy Post, and Bob Cunningham. In 2020 the group was extremely active in demanding justice for Breonna Taylor, with volunteers serving the unhoused, spreading political education, and bailing out protestors who were arrested when they occupied Jefferson Square Park in downtown Louisville. Even after forty years, Grupper remains active. He's just sorry he can't join the protests directly anymore but only offer administrative support.

Although he said he would never step foot in a synagogue again, Judaism has been a large part of Grupper's identity. He was national cochair of the New Jewish Agenda, a progressive organization focused on various social struggles, among them racism, anti-Semitism,

Jews with disabilities, environment, LGBTQ+ rights, nuclear weapons, the labor movement, and civil rights. One of the organization's more controversial stances has involved international issues.

Israeli-Palestinian relations have been a divisive issue among American Jews. Some strongly defend Israel. Some stand with the Palestinians. Some do their best to stick to domestic issues and largely avoid taking a stance at all.

But Grupper takes a strong stance for the rights of Palestinians. He said several times, "I am proud of who I am, but I'm not proud of what we have done." He said this solemnly and with what felt like a great responsibility. He has been involved in antiracism nearly his entire life, but as a white-presenting person, he recognizes his responsibility to fight white supremacy. He has never harmed a Palestinian, yet as a Jew he recognizes a responsibility to fight for them. When he said "we," I wondered whether he meant the general "we" or the two of us Jews. In 2009 he traveled to Gaza with several other local activists to join the Gaza Freedom Marchers protesting the attack by Israeli forces.

"We are our sister's and brother's keeper," said Grupper. "The life of a Palestinian fighting for a homeland must be as sacred and revered as that of a Jew."

To support the struggle in Jewish texts, Grupper cited Psalm 91, which he preferred to make gender-neutral: "I am with those in distress. I will release them, and I will honor them."

No matter if it's unpopular or controversial, or if the world he's lived in is not ready, Grupper has never shied away from following his conviction and taking a stand. As we wrapped up our conversation, he told me he was going to teach me a Yiddish phrase.

"Repeat after me," he said. "*Mit eyn . . .*"

"Mit eyn . . . ," I struggled to repeat.

". . . *tokhes . . .*"

". . . tokhes . . ." (I knew that one.)

". . . *ken men . . .*"

". . . ken men . . ."

". . . *nit tantsn . . .*"

". . . nit tantsn . . ."

". . . *af tsvey . . .*"

". . . af tsvey . . ."

". . . *khasenes.*"

". . . khasenes."

"You know what that means?"

"I do not."

"With one ass, you can't dance at two weddings."

Repairing the World

When protests had broken out in downtown Louisville after George Floyd was killed and while our community was still demanding justice for Breonna Taylor, it was Shabbat. I felt pulled to join and show solidarity in a Jewish way. I wanted those who were hurting to feel loved and supported.

Tikkun olam is a Jewish concept meaning "to repair the world." In its original context, it is best translated as "in the interest of public policy" and was used to advocate for the protection of those most in need of it, such as the slaves who needed freeing. Today, many Jews think of this concept as the impetus for their drive to pursue social justice.

I quickly fashioned a sign and crudely wrote a quote from Hillel that said, "If I am not for myself, who will be for me? If I am only for myself, what am I? And if not now, when?"

As I marched with my sign, several people approached me with an elbow bump. (Remember, it was a pandemic.) A few told me, "Shabbat shalom." Some just smiled. I felt it was important not only for people to see that I was with them but to see that I, as a Jewish person, was with them because Judaism drove me there.

The protests continued for months. In December some protestors set up a Christmas tree near the memorial for Breonna Taylor containing art, flowers, and signs. I made a menorah with the words "Tikkun Olam" on one side and "Black lives matter" on the other and, with the blessing of those occupying the square, placed it nearby with some candles.

Bend the Arc: Jewish Action Louisville, the organization I first joined as a Jeremiah fellow, strongly took the stance of supporting the movement for Black lives. Along with hundreds of other organizations and synagogues, we took out a full-page ad in the *New York Times* unequivocally declaring that Black lives matter. We had signs handy that read "Jews for Black Lives."

When I looked around at those protesting, I saw others driven by their religious conviction. Priests wearing clerical collars and crucifixes were saying "Catholics for Black lives" with their presence. Women wearing hijabs were saying "Muslims for Black lives." Clergy wearing pulpit robes were saying "Christians for Black lives."

Many Jews proudly quote Rabbi Abraham Joshua Heschel, who when he marched alongside Dr. Martin Luther King Jr. famously said he felt he was "praying with his feet." All around I see an interfaith service of people praying with their feet.

Fight Righteously

It is not necessary to have a religious affiliation to find inspiration from religious activists. The root of their conviction is largely in compassion for each other and conviction to pursue a more just world.

Answer the Call like the First Unitarian Church

- The church did not plan on becoming a safe house for protestors. But they saw an immediate need to show that Black Lives Matter was not just a sign on the front of the church, it was a conviction in the hearts of their congregation.
- Be willing to respond to those in need with the resources you have available. Get creative, like the congregation scouring the cabinets for mac and cheese. Think about what you have to give and how you can help when asked.
- Mean what you say. Show your solidarity through actions.

Take a Stand like Ira

- Consider your identity and whether your ancestors have contributed to the oppression of others. Think about how you may have benefited from the oppression of others, even if you've fought hard for liberation. Begin an antiracist journey and never quit.
- Think of those fighting alongside you as your brothers, sisters, and nonbinary family. Look after one another and promote community safety. Show compassion and empathy to others, recognizing the different struggles others face.
- Like Ira says, you can't dance at two weddings with one ass, and you can't always take the stance of neutrality. You need to follow your conviction and stand for what is right, regardless of status quo.

FOUR

EDUCATION

The Teachers Strike Back

In 2018, when then-governor Matt Bevin was asked by a reporter to comment on the ongoing teachers strike, he said:

"You know how many hundreds of thousands of children were left home today? I guarantee you somewhere in Kentucky today a child was sexually assaulted that was left at home because nobody was there to watch them. I guarantee you today, a child was physically harmed or ingested poison because they were left alone because a single parent didn't have any money to take care of them."

A sitting governor blaming public school teachers for hypothetical poisonings and trauma was shocking, even coming from a governor who also referred to teachers as "thugs" and "selfish." The Democratic attorney general, Andy Beshear, quickly condemned the comments. Kentucky Democrats and Republicans passed resolutions denouncing his comments. Suddenly nearly every political public figure in Kentucky had to make a statement that they did not believe educators are indirectly responsible for the poisoning or abusing of children, and admonish Bevin as if they were kindergarten teachers themselves telling him that wasn't a very nice thing to say.

The response from the teachers was a bit more direct. They just warned that they would remember in November. And—spoiler alert—they did.

Educators' foray into full-blown political activism began when Governor Bevin proposed some budget cuts that would be disastrous for many public schools already struggling to survive. The budget would eliminate millions set aside for textbooks and other instructional materials. It also required school districts to cut their administrative costs by 12 percent for the proposed budget year. School officials quickly responded that these cuts would be unsustainable and they could no longer guarantee to provide their students with the education they require. Plus, they said, these cuts would especially be damaging to school districts in coal country, which already experiences high rates of poverty and low rates of higher education pursued.

Small school districts whose students numbered only in the hundreds said they were barely getting by under the previous budgets. Such a huge cut would be dire to their students. As for school districts with many students, such as Jefferson County Public Schools covering Louisville, they too said the budget cuts would significantly affect their programs and leave them scrambling to find alternatives to meet the needs of their students.

Jefferson County Public Schools officials did concede that they had money in reserve, which might allow them to weather the storm. But they were concerned about other districts that did not have such emergency funds. Governor Bevin attacked districts such as JCPS for having money in reserve while the commonwealth grappled with a budget crisis. He also scolded Fayette County and JCPS in particular for having employees making more than $100,000 annually, and suggested that those employees—often principals, assistant principals, coun-selors, nurses, and psychologists—should be the focus of budget cuts. (Bevin, by the way, last reported his net worth as between $15.5 million and $60.6 million.)

Many of the cuts to education were general, forcing schools to decide which teachers to lay off or which sala-ries could be reduced. But some of the cuts were very spe-cific, such as the cut to JCPS's teenage parent programs serving pregnant teens and teenage parents by providing resources on how to balance education and new parent-hood. Only 50 percent of teenage mothers receive a high school diploma by age twenty-two. However, the teenage parent program boasts a 97 percent graduation rate.

Teachers decried these cuts and protested the changes, claiming it was a bad deal for everyone involved. It hurt students, teachers, and school administrators by severely straining resources. Schools already operating on a bare minimum budget would be completely broke, especially in the coal districts, in which local revenues had already fallen with the decline of the coal industry.

Governor Bevin didn't stop at just making teachers' jobs more difficult by reducing their already limited resources. He went after their pensions. Kentucky teachers have pension plans on which they are largely dependent for their retirement, as they're not eligible for Social Security. Bevin's proposed legislation mostly affected new teachers. The plan would reduce their benefits, such as the number of sick days that could be counted toward retirement. It required teachers to work longer before becoming eligible for retirement. Governor Bevin sold the proposal as a "hybrid" plan, less of a traditional pension and closer to a 401k model. Also, school districts were expected to contribute. The Kentucky Education Association referred to the pension bill as a "retaliatory effort" in response to teacher protests from the previous year. The largest teachers' union in the commonwealth called out the governor for going after teachers' pensions just because he was petty.

Personally, I find the union's allegation of pettiness pretty plausible. While Bevin was governor, I happened to notice that his official Twitter account blocked me. This was especially strange because, while I've criticized public officials, I've never even interacted with Bevin's account. It was just a preemptive block.

The pension plan wasn't the best even before Governor Bevin proposed making it worse. It was one of the worst-funded in the nation, and it's one of the few bipartisan issues that lawmakers can at least agree needs to be fixed.

Teachers in the commonwealth were furious about the proposed changes and warned that these could discourage prospective teachers from joining the profession at a time when more were desperately needed. They said a pension was a promise, and this was something so many teachers bet their careers on. They couldn't imagine this benefit not being available while teaching continues to become more and more difficult.

Additionally, the bill proposed restructuring the board managing those pensions. The Kentucky Education Association, a union representing almost 30,000 members, has been able to nominate four board members to help oversee the pension process. But under Bevin's bill, their representation would have been cut to only one board member.

Thousands of Kentucky teachers decided to strike, calling the demonstration a "sickout." At least eight districts, including the largest counties, Jefferson and Fayette, had to close for four days over the course of two weeks, as there weren't enough teachers or substitute teachers to carry on.

Brandy Brewer, a Jefferson County Public Schools teacher specializing in moderate and severe disabilities, left her classroom and joined her fellow teachers at the Capitol.

"I was motivated to protest at the Capitol mainly because of a desire to see that educators were being heard by legislators," said Brandy. "But more importantly I was there to make certain that special education students, special education teachers, and special education families were heard. Particularly because the population of students that I worked with were, in so many terms, voiceless."

Many political leaders promoted the idea that teachers were neglecting their students, while they themselves neglected to address the tremendous stress teachers in Kentucky face as they stretch their salaries to supply their classrooms and bring work home well after the bell rings. According to Brandy, teachers are expected to provide more while their funding is consistently cut.

"It's commonly misunderstood that teachers have the summers off and therefore are paid a certain amount of money over the course of their working months and that should not be deviated from," said Brandy. "In reality, teachers, educators, administrators all work tirelessly throughout the entire year. Do they get off at four o'clock? On paper. Does that work extend beyond their work hours? Yes. Does this translate into more hours worked than the regular forty-hour work week? Yes. Is that without additional compensation? Yes. These issues and issues relating to retirement and funding of public education are reasons for my participation in Frankfort."

Mobilized by the grassroots teachers' group KY 120 United, the pension flu hit teachers several times. Instead of watching *The Price Is Right* and sipping chicken noodle soup, the teachers protested at the Capitol wearing their red shirts. ("Red for Ed," very teacher-like to come up with a clever catchphrase for their attire.) They held signs asking, "Do we need to have a bake sale to fund this?" and "How can we put our students first when you put teachers last?" Some signs also included demands such as "Don't make me use my teacher voice" and the reminder "A pension is a promise."

The Red for Ed movement didn't just occur in the Bluegrass. Starting in 2018, teachers were organizing strikes in large numbers, similarly showing up in red attire to their state capitols. The strikes were sparked by budget cuts, low salaries, and decreases in employee benefits. Teachers also rejected proposals that they believed favored private schools over public schools, such as school choice and school vouchers.

Some of the strikes yielded some of the results the teachers demanded. In Arizona, 20,000 teachers protested for just about one week and successfully gained a 20 percent salary raise. Many states saw salary increases, education budgets restored to previous numbers, increased public school funding, and even reduction in class sizes. Almost every large-scale teacher protest resulted in an increase in education pay and funding . . . except in Kentucky.

Teachers in Kentucky continued to call in with the pension flu, showing up at the Capitol instead of school. Governor Bevin continued to insult them and accuse them of causing terrible tragedies with their absences, such as the death of a seven-year-old accidentally shot by his sibling on a day when school was closed by strikes. Pretty much anytime Governor Bevin was asked for comment about the ongoing battle with teachers over education funding or pensions, he used the opportunity to snub them.

Later in a gubernatorial debate, Bevin was asked about the accusations he had directed at teachers. His characterizing of the teachers as throwing a "temper tantrum" and as being "remarkably selfish" and having a "thug mentality" had become infamous. When he was asked if he regretted any of his cruel comments, he said, "I regret nothing that I have ever said about an educator. Nothing." Ouch.

Another aficionado of name-calling and mudslinging, Donald Trump, endorsed Bevin the night before the election, although he also called Bevin a pain in the ass.

Throughout the strikes, Attorney General Beshear served as an ally to the teachers and demonstrated sympathy for their plight. He filed lawsuits challenging Bevin's proposals in court, including when Bevin tried to subpoena schools for lists of teachers who participated in the sickouts. When the teachers came to the Capitol to strike, Beshear rushed to greet them. He shouted his support to large crowds on the steps of the Capitol. He spoke to individual teachers gathering in the annex to show their opposition.

For teachers, Andy Beshear was the true antithesis to Bevin. He not only opposed the cuts they viewed as disastrous, proposed by a governor that bullied them, but Beshear also just seemed really nice and wholesome. As many Kentuckians learned from watching his daily five-o'clock briefings delivering the latest updates on the COVID-19 pandemic, he has a very calming and kind presence that almost reminds you of a younger Mr. Rogers with a slight twang. I'd bet he enjoys dad jokes and going to bed at ten. Then Beshear really sealed the deal with teachers by choosing Jacqueline Coleman, an educator, as his running mate.

As part of Beshear's campaign for governor, teachers led "Bevin is a bully" events highlighting some of his most egregious comments. They hoped voters would be bothered by the simple fact that, at the very least, Bevin didn't seem like a very nice guy. He didn't exude southern hospitality. He certainly didn't seem as nice as good ol' Andy. Regardless of political affiliation, teachers volunteered to make phone calls, knock on doors, and do everything they could to charm voters in the same way they had been charmed by Beshear.

Although Beshear certainly charmed the teachers by taking the time to listen to why they chose to protest at the Capitol instead of teaching, and although they more closely aligned with his proposed policies, his most redeeming political quality was that he wasn't Matt Bevin. The gubernatorial campaign between Bevin and Beshear reminds me a bit of the bit in *Hamilton* after Schuyler is defeated by Aaron Burr and Alexander Hamilton confronts Burr.

Hamilton: No one knows who you are or what you do.
Burr: They don't need to know me. They don't like you.

Well, Kentuckians did not like Bevin. He held the title of Most Unpopular Governor in America, and at the height of the sickouts he had a 57 percent disapproval rating. To be sure, no matter how harsh the cuts may have been, many Kentuckians agreed with Bevin as far as policies were concerned. After all, this is a fiery-red commonwealth with many clinging fiercely to fiscal conservatism. Bevin claiming to save taxpayers money was appealing, even if it meant the cuts were coming from education.

What many voters didn't like was the rhetoric. They often said they agreed the pensions needed to be fixed, but they didn't like the way Bevin handled it. They didn't like that he seemed just plain mean.

How can we put our students first when you put teachers last?

The election between Beshear and Bevin became the closest since 1899. Beshear defeated Bevin by barely 5,000 votes, which equated to 0.37 percent of the total. Less than one-half of one percent determined the election. Voter turnout was especially high, which many believed was further evidence of the passion Kentuckians had to oust Bevin.

After Beshear was declared the winner and next governor of Kentucky, he addressed teachers directly in his victory speech:

"To our educators, this is your victory. Your courage to stand up and fight against all the bullying and name-calling helped galvanize our entire state."

The teachers continue to fight proposed budget cuts and other measures that could hinder their ability to provide their students with the best possible education. But their ally is now in the governor's mansion, and the union says their foray into political activism has just begun.

Decoding Functional Illiteracy

When it comes to ranking states on education, taking into account such factors as the quality of the education and the percentage of residents holding higher education degrees, Kentucky hasn't fared well. In the past several years, Kentucky is among the least educated.

One area where this is apparent is literacy. A staggering number of Americans are functional illiterates—some 43 million, or roughly one in seven. This problem affects many facets of their lives. Functionally illiterate people are more likely to live in poverty, be incarcerated, and have less access to healthcare and a lower life expectancy. Not to mention, it greatly inhibits their daily lives.

Adult illiteracy affects our society as a whole as well. Those who are functionally illiterate lack some of the necessary skills to become engaged and informed members of the public. This issue disproportionately affects Black, Latinx, and low-income families. When such a large number of Americans are functionally illiterate, it leads to economic loss through suppressed gross domestic product, more dependency on public assistance programs, and higher incarceration costs. In 2019, adult illiteracy was linked to an estimated cost of $428 billion.

You may be familiar with the idea of illiteracy, the complete inability to read, but not be as familiar with functional illiteracy. It's likely, though, that you know someone or have interacted with someone who qualifies as functionally illiterate. People who are functionally illiterate *can* read but are extremely limited in what they comprehend. They can read receipts with short words and remember which items they purchased, making sense of them. But when it comes to tasks like applying for a job, handling paperwork for government programs such as Social Security, reading the newspaper, and

making the inferences necessary to comprehend it—
those tasks are difficult to impossible.

This severely impacts their independence, as they
have to either ask others to do a task like filling out a
form or risk filling it out incorrectly because they can't
quite understand it. Often those who are functionally
illiterate feel embarrassment and shame, although it's
not uncommon and the circumstances leading to these
difficulties may have been out of their control.

For many functionally illiterate adults, their struggles
with reading began as children. Reading disabilities like
dyslexia and other learning difficulties are often missed
after the prime diagnosis period before second grade. If a
child has little exposure to literature and language in the
home, that can deter reading success. Sometimes teachers
don't receive the training necessary to identify children at
risk of reading difficulties, and they slip through the
cracks without getting the help they need.

The best way to fight illiteracy in adulthood is to teach
literate children. By looking for signs of struggle, getting
them help when needed, and promoting a love of reading,
more cases of functional adult illiteracy can be prevented.

The big factor in determining whether someone is
functionally illiterate is the activity required in their

daily lives. Someone in a developing country may be considered functionally literate because they're able to read what they need to read to complete their tasks, usually manual labor, and their low reading ability isn't much of a hindrance. But when they move to a developed country and suddenly they have to deal with a bureaucratic world of forms, job applications, maps, and complicated math at the grocery store, they no longer have the reading abilities to function normally. So they have shifted into being functionally illiterate under their new circumstances.

When industries evolve and jobs disappear, workers are left scrambling for new jobs that usually require more advanced skills. When someone loses a coal-mining job, sometimes the skill set that had been adequate their entire lives is actually functional illiteracy. Agricultural jobs often yield the same results, suddenly leaving former farmers not only looking for work but having an especially difficult time with limited reading abilities.

Richard L. Witherlite, executive director of a nonprofit serving the poor in Pineville, Kentucky, told a reporter from the *New York Times* in 2000: "A boy could quit school at a young age and make a good living. Then through the generations kids thought, 'Dad made it without an education, so I can make it.' That was O.K. as long as the coal mines were here."

The Louisville-based nonprofit Decode Project addresses the inequalities in education. We know that functional illiteracy affects Black, Latinx, and low-income families more than most, and we also know that early intervention in school is one of the best ways to prevent it. So that's where this nonprofit keeps its focus with its "Equity in Education" slogan and its mission of ensuring that all children have equitable access to resources, no matter where they live.

At the Decode Project they understand the importance of achieving literacy early for the students to go on to lead fulfilling lives and make worthwhile contributions to society. They prioritize approaching education in an unbiased, evidence-based, antiracist way that promotes the best environment for all children to learn and love reading.

Their method is fairly simple. They train literacy mentors using a structured approach that helps students learn phonemic awareness, sight words, spelling, building vocabulary, and identifying story ideas. This ensures that the students completely understand what they're learning to read. When children show signs of reading difficulties like dyslexia or are not reading at the appropriate grade level, mentors address the issue so the students can adapt and grow their skills. The Decode Project has a network of literacy advocates who contribute to workshops and who offer resources and support not only to educators but also to caregivers and community agencies. This better ensures that all children have access to the support they need to succeed.

The Decode Project webpage states:

> Reading is an essential skill for academic achievement as well as personal growth and development. It is our belief that literacy is vital to improving our community as a whole. We must prepare all children to confidently follow their natural curiosities and passions in life so they can grow up to educate, understand, inspire, and transform the world around them. This begins with the ability to read.

Another nonprofit, the Bluegrass Literacy Project, is led by students who aim to improve literacy in the commonwealth primarily by fostering a love for language.

They offer free workshops on etymology, the study of the origins of words and the way their meanings have changed throughout history.

The focus for the workshops is on the etymology of root words, because this is the most effective way to learn and retain vocabulary. A strong vocabulary leads to improved communication skills overall—listening, reading, speaking, writing. So it helps foster functional literacy as all these communication tasks become so much more feasible to accomplish.

The Bluegrass Literacy Project also sponsors the Scripps Spelling Bee throughout Kentucky and Indiana. This spelling bee is not like what you remember from your elementary school. This is the Olympics of spelling bees. The competition airs on ESPN and sounds as mentally challenging as a tennis match with Serena Williams would be physically challenging.

Here's a sample of some of the winning words from previous competitions. Familiar with any?

- "Feldenkrais." Oh? Don't know that one? Well, that's the exercise therapy pioneered by Israeli engineer Moshe Feldenkrais of course.

- How about "erysipelas"? That's a bacterial infection of the superficial layer of the skin. A common infection, but not a common word.
- "Appoggiatura," maybe? That's a grace note performed before a note of the melody and falling on the beat.

I not only never heard of that last word, I barely understand the definition. The organizers of this spelling bee basically comb the dictionary for the most difficult, off-the-wall words they can find to use in competition. And this is a children's competition!

The founder of the Bluegrass Literacy Project is a bright-eyed child herself. Tara Singh describes herself as a chocoholic, bibliophile, and linguaphile—a lover of words. (No kidding!) Singh qualified for her first Scripps Spelling Bee in 2013 when she was—wait for it—only seven years old. She's since returned to the annual spelling bee stage several times and has placed in the top ten competitors. She is a National Classical Etymology Exam gold medalist, which I had no idea was a thing.

Tara really, really loves language, and with the Bluegrass Literacy Project she uses this love to impassion others to challenge themselves and thrive in literacy.

Of course, being in a competition on national television and winning big trophies is in itself enticing for word-loving students. Plus, the ability to quickly spell nearly any word could prove to be a unique party trick that would pay off during the college years. But how, you may be wondering, does this affect literacy in practice? How could a national spelling bee help combat the functional illiteracy facing many Kentuckians?

Well, the national organization behind the big spelling bee, Scripps, is focused on all areas that literacy touches, promoting literacy across the board. One especially topical area is news literacy, or the ability to determine news credibility. People learn how to recognize which news sources are factual and which stories they can trust. The Bluegrass Literacy Project is striving to teach others that a story shared from the website definitelynotfakenews.net should not be trusted and definitely should not be shared for others to consume the misinformation.

The danger of fake news manifested itself through the attack on the United States Capitol, which had been breached by right-wing extremists on January 6, 2021. The threat to our democracy and physical danger to lawmakers, Capitol Police, and other federal employees was fueled by conspiracy theories and misinformation. Five people died and more than 140 were injured.

I can't help but think of Ashli Babbitt, one of the lives lost on that day. Babbitt served in the air force for fourteen years, and as she struggled with the transition to civilian life, she immersed herself in politics and the latest news. Unfortunately, the news sources she clung to were not credible. She followed the allure of QAnon, the far-right conspiracy theory peddler that promotes the idea that Donald Trump is America's great hope and any detractors are cannibalistic Satanists. No, really!

Babbitt was killed by a police officer as she was wearing a Trump flag around her neck as a cape and attempting to enter the Capitol through a broken window. She did not recognize that what she was consuming as factual news was just a series of ludicrous ideas invented by some malevolent swindler. She thought she was acting to reinstate an elected president and prevent the elitist Satan-worshipping pedophiles from taking power. She believed the lies so strongly, it cost her life.

This was far from the first time fake news caused real harm. Alex Jones of Infowars was notorious for spreading some of the most heinous lies. He spread the flagrant falsehood that the Sandy Hook elementary school shooting, which resulted in the deaths of twenty children, was just a hoax. As a result, his listeners harassed and threatened people they believed to be crisis actors, but who were actually grieving parents. Some parents were forced to go into hiding, wear disguises, or move.

Fake news and conspiracy theories are often crafted to be alluring, and it is sometimes difficult to determine their credibility unless you have developed the skills to do so. This gets especially tricky in the age of clickbait headlines and online news consumption. Determining which news sources are factual is necessary to function in our daily lives. But the inability to critically examine which news sources and bits of information are factual is a symptom of functional illiteracy.

Having so many people lacking the necessary literacy skills to function effectively affects our entire society. It not only harms the individual directly, but it also hurts all of us indirectly.

In Kentucky, functional illiteracy often runs in the family. It's difficult to break the cycle. When children don't have parents regularly reading to them, access to books, and reading habits to emulate, that's a major risk factor for future functional illiteracy. But if those children are given all the resources necessary to foster a true love and appreciation for language and literature, their reading skills can help them throughout their academic and future professional lives. Plus, they may be less likely to join a death cult and storm the Capitol. So it's a real win-win for everyone.

Promote Equitable Education

- Follow the courageous example of the teachers who stood up for themselves and their students to ensure they could do their jobs effectively.
- Be strategic. The teachers didn't get the policy changes they demanded and certainly not the respect they deserved from the politicians in power. So they voted them out. If your original avenue for change isn't working, shift to another one.
- Just as the Decode Project practices inclusivity, make sure no one is left behind and your activism lifts everyone.
- Follow your passions and allow them to inspire you to make a difference. Take the example of Tara Singh, a child with an insatiable love of words who is using this passion to promote literacy.

FIVE

POLITICAL REPRESENTATION

THROUGHOUT THE HOLLOWS of eastern Kentucky and the urban areas of Louisville and Lexington there are thriving, diverse Black, Jewish, Latinx, Muslim, LGBTQ+, and progressive groups. Some outsiders dismiss Kentucky on the basis of outdated stereotypes, but the people of Kentucky know these are not true. Sure, the commonwealth is especially Caucasian, even more than the rest of the United States. But Black, Indigenous, and People of

Color exist here! They live here, they hold powerful positions, they lead movements.

But not so much in the Kentucky General Assembly.

The Kentucky House and Senate are overwhelmingly Republican, holding massive power. The State Senate currently has 29 Republicans and 9 Democrats, while the State House has 75 Republicans and only 25 Democrats. This majority has made it virtually impossible for the state Democrats to pass any remotely progressive bill, while some pretty asinine bills tend to skate through.

Here's one example. In the aftermath of Breonna Taylor's killing, the people of Kentucky, and much of the world, demanded justice. Thus far, justice has not come in the form of any police officers involved in her killing being charged for her death. Many activists and legal experts shifted strategy to focus on one factor related to her death, no-knock warrants. These warrants allow police officers to storm someone's residence unannounced and can cause confusing and dire consequences, as we've seen. A bill named Breonna's Law has been introduced in the Kentucky House, but so far it hasn't gained the traction necessary to move forward into law.

Meanwhile, Republicans in the legislature have taken the opportunity to respond to Taylor's tragic death and the outrage expressed in Kentucky in response. Republican Senator Danny Carroll, a retired police officer, examined the issues and thought to himself, "Ah, I see the real problem here. People saying mean things to cops!" So Senator Carroll introduced a bill that designates insulting a police officer as disorderly conduct, a Class B misdemeanor, if someone specifically

> accosts, insults, taunts, or challenges a law enforcement officer with offensive or derisive words, or by gestures or other physical contact, that would have a direct tendency to provoke a violent response from the perspective of a reasonable and prudent person.

Even if you're not a revered constitutional scholar, you may rightly have a concern that this bill may conflict with one of those big amendments. (Psst, it's the first one.) You also may be rightly worried that "reasonable and prudent people" are too quick to turn to violence.

It's offensive. It's absurd. It's not just an issue of not hearing the people, it's blatantly choosing to ignore them.

The average Kentucky representative is a white, male, Christian baby boomer and is likely to be a business owner or attorney. The demographics of the General Assembly are:

- 83 percent male, 17 percent female
- 91 percent white, 5 percent Black
- 92 percent Christian, 1 percent non-Christian

The crowd at Cracker Barrel on a Sunday afternoon looks more diverse than the Kentucky General Assembly.

From birth, Attica Scott seemed destined for activism. Her parents named her after the uprising, some twenty weeks before she was born, when inmates took over the state prison in Attica, New York, and demanded better living conditions and political rights.

In 2016 Scott became the first Black woman elected to the Kentucky House of Representatives in nearly twenty years. She now proudly calls herself a "reptivist," balancing her ongoing political activism with her role as an elected representative. She joins ongoing protests calling for racial justice but then follows that with introducing legislation that advances racial equity. She uses the political power she has to address issues facing the communities she represents. It doesn't sound like a radical concept, but it's currently scarce in the state legislature.

Continuing the tradition of manifesting power through powerful names, Attica Scott named her son Advocate and her daughter Ashanti, which has African connotations of graciousness and Arabic connotations of warlike aggression. Scott envisioned a warrior princess in choosing the name. During the protests in the aftermath of Breonna Taylor's killing, teenage Ashanti demonstrated beside her mother, which also meant suffering through the sting of tear gas and being arrested.

As a single mother, Representative Scott intimately understands the difficulties mothers face. She continues to work full-time in public health while serving in the legislature. When I asked her to clarify that, she laughed and said that the $21,000 representatives make isn't going to pay her rent. She doesn't own huge businesses or possess inherited wealth to supplement her income like some of her colleagues. She has to work.

Her background as a mother and public health professional has guided her to sponsor legislation like the Maternal Care Access and Reducing Emergencies Act. Maternal mortality is a horrific problem in the United States, with around seven hundred women dying every year. Instead of improving, the rate has gotten even worse, rising by 26 percent between 2000 and 2014. Women of color are three times more likely to die from childbirth or pregnancy-related conditions than white women.

The bill is designed to keep moms healthy to have healthy babies. It provides more oversight to prevent infant mortalities. Because Representative Scott recognizes the part structural racism plays in maternal healthcare, it also requires implicit bias training to improve the experience and outcomes for mothers of color. It also expands Medicaid to pay for doula services, which have been shown to greatly improve the birth experience. Scott also sponsored legislation that would reduce the unnecessary cost of necessary items by removing the tax on baby products such as diapers, wipes, and bottles.

The experience of an elected state representative protesting police brutality and then being hit with tear gas and arrested and charged with a felony caught attention outside the commonwealth. Headlines like "Kentucky State Rep. Attica Scott, Who Authored Breonna's Law, Arrested at Louisville Protests" inspired people nationwide to ask, "What the hell is going on in Kentucky?" When I spoke with Representative Scott about the experience and the collective trauma Black women have experienced throughout the past year of protests and judicial heartache, she said:

"Well, Kentucky is cruel to Black women, *period*, very cruel. And the legislature is no different. So things have been hard for Black women every single year, and last year—last year was painful.

"It was painful because we were out there on the front lines for justice for Breonna Taylor, and I serve a district that literally is, like, forty-nine percent white and Black. On the white part of the district, we had a protest and police were just kind of hanging out here, didn't say or do anything. Then immediately I go downtown, which is mostly Black people, and it's tear gas. Violence. All the arrests. And that's what happened to other people. It was beyond heartbreaking. I don't know if there are words for what I feel like I experienced."

I knew exactly the disparity she meant. It was undeniable. The largest protest I had attended was the first Women's March of 2017 in Washington, D.C. It was also the largest single-day protest in American history, with more than 200,000 people in D.C. alone. We marched through the streets, chanted, held signs, all the standard protest stuff. I vividly remember police officers directing traffic and even high-fiving protestors as they passed.

Naively, I first celebrated the warm welcome by the police and the fact that not a single arrest was made. I didn't immediately think that maybe that was because most of the marchers looked like me, and no matter how many white women in pink knitted hats gather, they're unlikely to be met with tear gas and riot gear.

When I marched in the streets of my community, it was not unlike that first Women's March. We held signs and chanted. At its height, there were hundreds of protestors. But this time Black voices were leading the chants, and most of the crowd was Black. There were no high fives from the police. I never thought to google whether it's water or milk that neutralizes tear gas until I protested with a majority Black crowd. (It's water; milk helps with the pepper balls.) When police approached the crowd in line formation, holding shields and riot gear covering their faces, the crowd would anxiously await what was to come. Tear gas? Rubber bullets? Pepper balls? Mass arrests?

It was chilling.

Attica Scott knows her district—the 41st, which encompasses much of the Louisville area—and its demographics. While she's finally representing issues BIPOC face, and especially Black women, she's also mindfully fighting for issues facing *all* people in her district.

"There are so many people across Kentucky, not only in the district that I represent, not only in Louisville, but across Kentucky, who deserve to have people who are using their voice and their position to speak up on human rights and social justice," said Representative Scott. "To really advocate for fairness and equity and freedom. All of Kentucky deserves that.

"I remember my first session here in 2017, young white women were here doing their grassroots lobbying from eastern Kentucky. They stopped by my office to say, 'Thank you for being the representative we wished we had.' At that moment, I was reminded of why I need to be here. It wasn't only for the Black babies in the West End of Louisville where I live. It's important for everyone to see a Black woman advocating for all of us."

Currently the Kentucky General Assembly is extremely white, extremely male, and does not accurately represent the people of Kentucky. So when I asked Representative Scott what someone could do to become politically engaged and increase representation, she was clear.

"RUN," she said. "I tell folks who've been on the front lines for justice for Breonna Taylor, run! Run for local office. Run for state office. You deserve to be in D.C. You deserve to join a lot of us. You know what you want to do. You deserve to be a state representative. I'm just keeping this seat warm for you.

"Work on a campaign with people who you believe in, who you share values with. If you don't want to run for office? OK! But support people who are putting themselves out there on the line and who are opening themselves up to be vulnerable to all kinds of attacks, and support them. Put your energy behind them."

With such an overwhelming Republican majority and a slew of bills damaging to progressive causes likely to be passed, many activists are feeling nervous and pessimistic about the upcoming sessions. But Attica Scott is feeling energized and proud of the progress that has been made so far to increase political representation in the commonwealth. While other activists consider how difficult it may be to change the future of Kentucky politics, she says they're already doing it.

"I feel like we're already working to change the face of Kentucky politics. We have our first-ever Indian immigrant serving here in the statehouse, Representative Kulkarni. Now two Black women are serving in the statehouse. We've got activists who are running for office at the local and state level. People who are like me—who work full-time and have to work full-time, working folks—are raising families, running for office, and winning. We are changing the face of Kentucky politics.

"We're not allowing anyone to run over us anymore and, you know, feel like we have to bow down to white saviors, or the Speaker of the House, or the President of the Senate. No. We're saying we have the right to demand the best for us—not just the least for us, the best for us. And that's exactly what's happening."

Representation from the Hood to the Holler

Charles Booker, once Kentucky's youngest Black lawmaker, has always been a standout. In late 2019 I attended an interim session of the Kentucky statehouse advocating for a gun violence prevention bill. There had been a lot of speculation and chatter about whether Representative Booker would run in the Democratic primary for United States Senate and strive to take down Senate majority leader Mitch McConnell. So I was excited to have a chance to see him in action and get a sense of who he was.

Several things stood out to me. First of all, um, he was there. This was an interim session, no voting was being done, and there were lots of empty seats. But Representative Booker not only attended but was actively listening, asking thoughtful questions, and taking notes. After the session ended, instead of rushing out evading reporters, he took the time to speak with his constituents. Even odder, he didn't need any introductions! I watched him give a little side hug to a gun violence survivor, Terrell Williams, and it was clear he already knew the story of how Williams was shot in his district, and so he just greeted him with a little "Hey Terrell." He was gracious and thanked everyone for coming. Although he wasn't directly involved with the bill, he had been a needed champion for gun violence prevention in the statehouse. Booker lost five family members to gun violence, and his passion toward the issue was evident.

In my conversation with Kentucky Equal Justice Center attorney Ben Carter, we discussed some of the political issues facing Kentucky with the heavily weighted Republican General Assembly likely to block progressive policies, as well as the discouraging political moves that have made the need for change so apparent.

"It's not just a political problem," said Carter. "It's at its core sort of a spiritual endeavor to change the way we see the world and our place in it. So, that work doesn't happen overnight. It doesn't happen in a generation, probably. But people like Charles are exactly the kind of people who, in a moment, tear down some of those false walls that we've built up around each other."

Booker later officially announced he was running for the Senate. Amy McGrath had announced her candidacy earlier. As her commercials highlighted, she was a Marine, fighter pilot, and mom, and she stood wearing bomber jackets and in front of jets like a Kentucky reboot of *Top Gun*. But McGrath's biggest asset was that she had announced first, so for months she was presented as the candidate running against McConnell. Liberals from all across the nation threw money at her, not because they cared too much about her policies or even lived in Kentucky, but because they just really hated McConnell. She raised $46 million.

Booker, born and raised in Louisville, graduated from a local public high school and then from the University of Louisville's law school. When protests erupted over racial violence, Booker joined them. Just as I witnessed the previous year, he showed that he cared and shared concerns, and most of all he took the time to listen.

As a child, Booker was diagnosed with type 1 diabetes, and he has vivid memories of needing to ration his insulin due to the inability of his family to pay the rising costs. Personal experiences like these influenced his support of universal healthcare.

He also embraced other progressive positions—a Green New Deal to combat climate change, criminal justice reform, universal basic income, to name a few. Energized by his ideas and sincerity, Kentuckians invested in his campaign, giving both time and money. He raised more than one million dollars and proudly pointed out that the donations came from some regular folks offering what small amounts they had to give.

You deserve a government that accounts for your humanity.
—Charles Booker

Before the election, his campaign had gained national attention, with progressives rooting for him well outside the commonwealth. The largest newspapers in Kentucky, the *Courier Journal* and the *Lexington Herald-Leader*, both endorsed him. Advocacy organizations including the Working Families Party and the Sunrise Movement supported him. He had warm endorsements from Elizabeth Warren, Bernie Sanders, Alexandria Ocasio-Cortez, Ayanna Pressley, Tom Steyer, Julian Castro, former

Kentucky secretary of state Alison Lundergan Grimes, and even Susan Sarandon. Progressives were salivating at the idea of Booker beating McConnell.

However, he didn't quite get the chance. McGrath beat Booker in the primary, taking 45.4 percent of the vote compared to Booker's 42.7 percent. (McGrath later lost to McConnell in a quite decisive race.)

In Booker's concession speech he said:

"Don't ever let someone tell you what's impossible. Don't ever give up on your dreams for a brighter future. No matter where you are from, what color your skin is, how much money you have, who you love, what pronoun you use, whether you walk or use a wheelchair, or what you believe—you matter. You deserve a government that accounts for your humanity. From this moment on, let's take the frustration we feel and commit to fighting for change like never before. Let's dedicate ourselves to the work of beating Mitch so that we can get him out of the way. Yes, I would love to be your nominee, but know I'm still by your side. Thank you for giving me this opportunity. Kentucky, I love you. From the hood to the holler."

After his primary loss, he took the opportunity while he had Kentucky's attention to launch a new organization with the mission of fighting for "political power to heal, transform, and build communities rooted in love and justice, rather than hate." As a man of faith, Booker says he believes in showing up authentically with an inclusive message, speaking to the challenges Kentuckians face.

After the dismantling of Jim Crow laws in the 1950s and 1960s, Republicans launched a profoundly racist plan to win elections. Consistent with most racist ideas, it was not very clever or complicated. Dubbed the "southern strategy," the plan was to increase political support among white southern voters by appealing to racist notions about Black southerners.

In the late 1960s, according to White House chief of staff H. R. Haldeman, Richard Nixon "emphasized that you have to face the fact that the whole problem is really the Blacks. The key is to devise a system that recognized this while not appearing to." Whew. I'm not sure what is more offensive—the reference to "the Blacks," calling an entire race of people "the problem," or the methodical evil in subtly concealing this blatant racism. The way this strategy worked in practice was promoting states' rights, opposing voters' rights and forced busing, and pretty much Ronald Reagan's entire campaign.

With Hood to the Holler, Booker calls for a new southern strategy that rejects the ugliness that has divided the South for too long. Here's some of the strategy Hood to the Holler is working toward:

- Removal of barriers to democratic participation
- Empowerment of a more reflective democracy
- Engagement of all Kentuckians (from, as the name evokes, the hood to the holler)
- Breaking down of racial justice barriers
- Ending of generational poverty

Stacey Abrams spectacularly rebounded from a political loss and invested her time and talents into increasing political representation and combatting voter suppression in Georgia. Her efforts, along with grassroots organizers', paid off in a big way during the 2020 election when they helped secure Joe Biden's presidential victory and the election of two new Democratic senators. With Hood to the Holler's similar emphasis on increasing political representation, Booker is investing in Kentuckians as they invested in him and hoping for a similar payoff.

Fighting for the Right to Vote

In 1982 the University of Kentucky women's basketball team was on fire. The Lady Kats won the Southeastern Conference regular-season title and the league tournament. They lost in the inaugural women's NCAA tournament to the eventual national champions, Louisiana Tech, but ranked fourth in the nation the next season. Avid sports fans credit the 1981–1982 Lady Kats with forever influencing the future of the program. They were true pioneers of Kentucky women's basketball.

The team captain and one of the team's stars, Tayna Fogle, was a crowd favorite who stood out with her spunky personality and bright smile. She was known as a hometown heroine, born and raised in Lexington, where she shined on the court. She could think quickly, coming up with winning strategies at moments when they were needed most. The team won the championship game on her twenty-second birthday.

Fogle grew up, like many Kentuckians, in poverty.

"I was poor, but my mother never allowed us to know the whole story," Fogle told me. "I never knew I was poor because of the rich love that she gave us. Plus, you know, everybody on our block lived as we did, so we didn't know anything else. We all stood in the commodity line, we all went to the Pick 'n Save shoe store. We all wore hand-me-downs. There was no meat throughout the week except on Sundays, when we had chicken. And it's usually the chickens that were in our backyard, so we couldn't make friends with our chickens. I made the mistake of doing that, by the way."

She's now a mother of two, grandmother of eleven, and still has that warm personality and big smile that I can imagine so many basketball fans loved. She received a four-year scholarship to attend the University of Kentucky and graduated with a Bachelor of Arts degree in therapeutic recreation. But according to her, she never got the opportunity to fully utilize it.

Drug addiction affects poor communities of color more than most, and it affected Tayna Fogle too. She bounced checks at the local corner store and sold small amounts of cocaine to facilitate her addiction. She was selling a very small amount—small enough to fit under your fingernail, she said—and put it on a piece of paper for the buyer. What she didn't know was that the buyer was a confidential informant.

The informant turned Fogle in, and she was charged with drug dealing and check fraud. Each conviction carried a five-year sentence, and the judge ordered her to serve them consecutively. The imprisonment and aftermath made her dependent on public assistance to provide for herself and her family. She felt engulfed by the system.

"I was taken hostage by the system, and my children were collateral damage," said Fogle. "The state penal system was supporting me. Then the food stamp office, now called SNAP, was supporting my children, and my mother was raising them."

After serving her sentence, she actively sought a job. But the best she could find, given her criminal history, was at McDonald's. She shook her head, remembering scrubbing toilets at the fast-food chain and knowing it was all she could now do, even with a bachelor's degree. Not exactly what she had in mind.

She founded reentry programs, ministries, and training in counties throughout the commonwealth to help other people like herself reintegrate into society. She knew that just because someone may have had trouble with the law, that didn't mean that they didn't have goals, talents, and skills to offer. But they often needed some help navigating the complicated system, and they craved being treated with the dignity and respect that Fogle gave them.

"You know, I made some mistakes," she says. "But I'm not a mistake. All we want to do is get back to our dream, the dream we had before we committed the crime.

"Because of white Americans in the opiate crisis, they have reworked sentencing to make sure white Americans do not go to prison. Therefore they will not receive the felony offense we have struggled with. I think I've worked on the restoration of voting rights for twenty years now. For about twenty years we've been in the fight for those behind me.

"We have generational curses. I have two sons, who both have felonies. The system is broken. My family is broken! So many families get broken because of the system."

As Fogle is overtaken by emotion in telling her story, her colleague at the Poor People's Campaign, Pam McMichael, attempts to console and support her, which is especially difficult via virtual meeting. The pair have worked together on the Poor People's Campaign to fight systemic racism, poverty, the military industrial complex, and ecological devastation, as well as what they call the nation's distorted morality of religious nationalism. Even virtually, their friendship and mutual respect are obvious.

The Poor People's Campaign was originally born out of the vision of Dr. Martin Luther King Jr., who announced the organization's formation at a staff retreat for the Southern Christian Leadership Conference the year before he was killed. The vision was based on a revolution of values, and the conference was an appropriate place to announce the mission, as faith leaders have been a consistent presence in the group. The call from Dr. King is fundamentally the same today—the moral purpose of caring for one's neighbors and demanding justice for all.

The group believes a moral revival based on religious and/or constitutional values is necessary for the pursuit of justice and the strength of our democracy. The conditions that became consequences affecting Fogle's life are defiantly rejected by the Poor People's Campaign. They recognize that the United States is the richest nation in the world, and as such, they don't believe anyone in it should live in poverty or die as a result. They recognize the systemic racism that plays into keeping people in a cycle of economic oppression. They believe that poverty, economic inequality, and white supremacy are deeply intertwined.

One of the moral narratives that the campaign believes is pervasive and that it seeks to eliminate is the blaming of poor and oppressed people for their poverty and oppression. Fogle said she has made mistakes but is not a mistake. The Poor People's Campaign not only agrees that her history is not indicative of a moral failing that she must forever carry, but they also look deeper at the underlying issues that led to her criminal history. When they hold direct actions and events to discuss their goals publicly, they make sure that Fogle and others affected directly by these harmful policies have the mic.

"We change the moral narrative by changing the teller of the story," says Pam McMichael. "That's been a key part of the Poor People's Campaign. That's a key point, who is the teller of the story. So the bravery of Tayna and other people to tell their stories is really what has driven the Poor People's Campaign."

Kentucky has been only one of two states holding to a policy of permanent felony voter disenfranchisement. This harsh penalty disqualifies anyone convicted of a felony *for life*. Thousands and thousands of Kentuckians have been ineligible to vote due to this policy. Many leaders in the Poor People's Campaign rejoiced at Andy Beshear's gubernatorial victory, because he voiced the same moral principles they believe in so strongly and was ready to put those principles into action by restoring voting rights to Kentuckians with felony convictions.

Along with her work at the Poor People's Campaign, Fogle has been a Democracy Fellow with Kentuckians for the Commonwealth (KFTC) for much of her advocacy. KFTC is committed to the pursuit of true equality and representative democracy through nonviolent action, much like the Poor People's Campaign. The KFTC website describes their vision for Kentucky:

We are working for a day when Kentuckians—and all people—
enjoy a better quality of life.
When the lives of people and communities matter before profits.
When our communities have good jobs that support our families
without doing damage to the water, air, and land.
When companies and the wealthy pay their share of taxes
and can't buy elections.
When all people have health care, shelter, food, education, and other basic needs.
When children are listened to and valued.
When discrimination is wiped out of our laws, habits, and hearts.

*And when the voices of ordinary people
are heard and respected in our democracy.*

Fogle was introduced to KFTC leaders shortly after her release from prison. She felt empowered by the embrace of a group of people who didn't judge her and wanted to hear her story. After she served her time, she tenaciously worked to contribute and find her place in society. But she was shocked to discover that with her felony conviction, she had lost the right to vote.

"I can remember my mom teaching us how to vote," she said through tears. "I remember the stories—my grandmother died at a hundred and two, and I remember the stories that my granny, and my mom, used to tell us about how hard it was to vote, and how important it is to vote, and how many people died that look like me trying to vote. That's why we should always vote."

Many Kentuckians like Fogle have no idea they lost the right to vote with their felony convictions. It was a representative of KFTC who told Fogle she was now ineligible and helped explain the convoluted process of getting her rights restored. They directed her to her parole officer, who directed her to some forms. She wrote the required essay, paid the fees, produced character references. She said she didn't recognize it then, but she now sees how that process burdens people in poverty unable to pay the fees and those with low levels of literacy, who would have difficulty filling out the form and writing an essay. After some bureaucratic mix-ups, clerical errors, and delays, she eventually marched the application to the governor's office personally to ensure it landed in the right hands and her rights were restored.

When she struggled to find the correct polling place, she stopped and asked a police officer. (Which she said she could do because she was no longer running from the police.) The officer directed her to the correct place. When she made it inside, she said, she felt that familiar feeling of her mom taking her to the polls overwhelm her.

But the last time she voted, the process was completely different. She remembered pulling a big handle, much like you'd see on a slot machine in Las Vegas. But now everything was digital. There was a wheel, and she wasn't sure what to do. The person waiting to vote behind her grew impatient and asked her to hurry as she scrambled to decipher the new voting machine code. She threw the curtain back and exclaimed, "It has taken me thirteen years to vote, and you will wait, sir."

She asked a volunteer at the polling place to help and quickly got the instructions necessary to vote. Her hands shook with excitement so much, she had to also ask a volunteer to affix the "I voted!" sticker on her, which she couldn't wait to show to all her friends at KFTC. But her story is a typical example of the barriers disenfranchising people. Kentuckians for the Commonwealth help fill in the gaps left by the policy. They inform Kentuckians about their voting rights, help restore those rights if requested, educate voters about specifics on election day, and ensure their votes are counted.

When Governor Beshear issued an executive order restoring voting rights to 140,000 former felons in Kentucky, Fogle was proudly standing in the audience, watching him sign the document. She smiled brightly as she recalled the balloons and celebratory environment. But while she's proud of all the work they've done, she says there's much more to do, and she intends to take full advantage of the open-door policy Governor Beshear promised them.

There's also the immediate issue of the 140,000 Kentuckians who had their voting rights restored and . . . um, who's going to tell them? Many advocates have called the current system woefully inadequate, as it depends on a website that former felons would need to find and check to see if their rights were restored. The Poor People's Campaign, KFTC, and other advocacy groups scrambled to train volunteers to call voters. This has been a challenge, as those with a criminal history are likely to have inaccurate addresses and phone numbers, and be hesitant to speak to someone they don't know. But Fogle and others work tirelessly to let them know how valued their voices are and do everything possible to ensure they're heard.

Years after her release, Fogle was arrested again, but this time for protesting with the Poor People's Campaign, and more specifically, she said, singing arm-in-arm in the streets of Washington, D.C. Many were arrested, including the Poor People's Campaign cochair Reverend William Barber II, a Protestant minister in North Carolina and longtime political activist. Barber has spoken at the Democratic National Convention and has served as an authority on morality and civil rights. When Fogle talked of her arrest related to drug charges, she solemnly recalled the years she had lost. But when she recounted her arrest protesting with the Poor People's Campaign, she looked like she was recalling a pleasant memory. She said she was proud to be arrested with Reverend William Barber.

Reverend Barber's face may be familiar to you if you recall local news coverage in 2018 when the Poor People's Campaign was denied access to the Capitol in Frankfort. He angrily stood wearing a cross and his clerical robe as he argued with State Troopers near metal detectors. Fogle stood right behind him.

The group had come to the Capitol to protest work requirements for Medicaid, a plan then-governor Matt Bevin endorsed. About four hundred people attended the protest showing their opposition. But when they attempted to enter the building, they were stopped. Apparently a brand-new rule had been instituted stating that only two people could enter the Capitol at a time. I'm sure it had nothing to do with the Poor People's Campaign's planned protest and was just an inconvenient coincidence.

The image of many Black clergy and activists gathered by metal detectors as they prayed and sang, blocked by police from entering the Capitol, ironically juxtaposed with another image of white gun rights activists gathering in the Capitol holding their semiautomatic weapons above their heads. Not only was this strange because protestors had previously been told they could not enter the Capitol with umbrellas, lest these be used as a weapon.

But gun rights supporters wearing ski masks and military fatigues were instructed to walk around the metal detectors and were allowed to enter with actual weapons.

We celebrate the ideas of Dr. King and keep our kids home from school on the national holiday honoring his legacy. But when a group looking much like the Reverend Dr. King advocates for those same ideas, they're denied entry.

Still, voting rights activists stay focused on their mission to empower Kentuckians to tell their stories and exercise their rights to be heard.

Fogle is often reminded of a quote she heard from one of her favorite activists, Shelton McElroy of Louisville, who asked, "If the vote was not so important, why would they try so hard to keep us from doing it?"

Share Political Power and Empower the Powerless

- Take Attica Scott's advice and run for office if you're able. If you're not willing or able, support those who are, with your time and donations. Grassroots political support can go a long way.

- If you hold power, keep the seat warm like Representative Scott and be willing to share that power and pass it on to others willing to serve and make a difference.
- Take the time, like Charles Booker, to listen to the struggles and concerns of others.
- Follow Booker's example and look for opportunities to support coalitions that serve as an alternative to past institutions that have oppressed Kentuckians.
- Treat the disenfranchised with dignity and respect, like Pam McMichael. Be willing to pass the figurative mic and allow those affected directly to tell their stories.
- Use the story of Tayna Fogle to remind you never to take your right to vote for granted. Exercise your right and fight for the rights of all Kentuckians to be rightfully heard.

SIX

RACIAL JUSTICE

THE STREETS previously occupied by protestors demanding justice for Breonna Taylor had been taken over by military vehicles surrounded by dozens of police officers and National Guard members wearing military fatigues and riot gear, grasping assault weapons. On either side of the street, plywood blocked the windows of sub shops and federal buildings. Breonna Taylor had been shot down by police who barged into her home in the middle of the night. The investigation into her death, which revealed numerous missteps, poor record keeping, and actions that went against police training protocols, took months while activists pleaded for justice. In the end, none of the officers involved were charged in Taylor's death. After a grand jury decision that left protestors feeling justice had been denied, the city of Louisville looked prepared for war.

Illuminated by siren lights, the image of a bright young woman hung across the façade of a skyscraper with the words "Alberta's Louisville" alongside her profile. These banners, part of the Hometown Heroes program intended to promote civic pride, featuring some of Louisville's most famous—Oscar-winning actress Jennifer Lawrence, the fried chicken icon Colonel Sanders, and broadcast journalist Diane Sawyer, to name a few—were impossible to miss.

Alberta Odell Jones was a brilliant attorney, passionate civil rights activist, and trailblazing icon. She became one of the first Black women to pass the Kentucky bar. During the height of the civil rights movement, Alberta protested segregation and racial injustice, marching in the streets of Louisville and participating in the March on Washington of 1963 where Dr. Martin Luther King Jr. delivered his famous "I Have a Dream" speech to impassioned activists like Alberta. She strived to increase voter participation among the Black community, registering thousands. To ensure Black voters were properly educated on what to do when they entered a voting booth, she rented voting machines and taught them how to properly use them.

After graduating near the top of her class at Howard University, Alberta returned home to Louisville to practice law. She told the *Courier Journal* in early 1965:

> When I got back home a lot of people said, "You've got two strikes against you. You're a woman and you're a Negro."
>
> Yeah, but I've got one strike left, and I've seen people get home runs when all they've got left is one strike.

By the spring of 1965, the battle over the federal Civil Rights Act had been won and Alberta had become the first Black female prosecutor in the Commonwealth of Kentucky. By summer, she was murdered. By 2020, her image overlooked the battle for racial justice continuing to rage in the same streets she once marched, and her murder remains unsolved.

Alberta's Louisville today celebrates many victories in racial justice as a result of the tireless work of

Kentuckian activists. However, the fight for racial justice today is eerily similar to the fight when Ms. Jones marched the streets.

In Dr. King's *Letter from Birmingham Jail*, he wrote that specifically the South, the nation, and the world are in dire need of "creative extremists" who, in his view, like Jesus Christ fought for love, truth, and goodness. He went on to discuss the struggle the oppressor race had understanding the struggles of Black people and how they were even less likely to understand the strategic vision that involved rooting out injustice with strong, persistent, and determined action.

He expressed gratitude to the white allies in the South—"all too few in quantity, but . . . big in quality"—who understood the heart of the civil rights movement and dedicated their work to that vision. One of the six allies Dr. King singled out as allies recognizing the urgency of combatting segregation was Louisville-born Anne Braden.

Along with her husband Carl, Anne Braden understood and practiced the principles of antiracism decades before author Dr. Ibram X. Kendi brought the idea into the mainstream, or was even born. The Bradens not only supported desegregation and the civil rights movement;

they embarked on the deeply introspective journey of examining how they, as white people, were responsible for upholding a system that oppressed Black people. Then they committed to dismantling that system unlike anyone had before. Anne wrote in her memoir, *The Wall Between*:

> Either you find a way to oppose the evil, or the evil becomes part of you and you are part of it, and it winds itself around your soul like the arms of an octopus, . . . If I did not oppose it, I was . . . responsible for its sins.

The Bradens' love story began as they met in the newsroom of the *Courier Journal*. They not only shared a passion for their journalism careers but also shared views on trade unions and civil rights. By the early 1950s the couple had left their mainstream journalism careers to write for the interracial leftist labor movement via the Farm Equipment Workers union. (Who knew farm equipment could be so radical?) This was one of the first personal sacrifices the couple made for their convictions.

Anne had begun solidifying her role as a white ally fighting for racial justice by leading an effort to desegregate the hospitals in Kentucky. She was arrested for the first time in 1951 after she mobilized a large group of white southern women along with the Civil Rights Congress to go to Mississippi to protest the impending execution of Black southerner Willie McGee. The case of McGee's execution was viewed by civil rights activists as a heinous miscarriage of justice fraught with constitutional violations, Jim Crow–era missteps, and racist stereotypes.

The Bradens stood in direct defiance of the idea that southern whites opposed the civil rights movement, and this made them intensely unpopular. Due to their outspoken support of desegregation and civil rights activism, the couple had a reputation in the community that didn't earn them social invitations among their white southern neighbors, but it did garner propositions from Black Kentuckians in need.

Andrew and Charlotte Wade, a Black couple with a toddler and a baby on the way, had a dream of owning a home in a nice suburban neighborhood, and a house in the Louisville suburb of Shively was perfect—*House Hunters* approved. Well, except of course for the little snag that, under Jim Crow–era housing practices, the Wades couldn't purchase property. It wasn't illegal per se, but it wasn't probable that a Black family would be able to purchase a home in an all-white neighborhood, as the Wades discovered when they were turned down by real estate agent after real estate agent who refused to help the family. Finally, one agent said the only way the Wades could possibly own a home outside the unofficial and yet clearly recognized line of segregation would be for a white person to purchase it and transfer the property.

So the Wades asked their friends the Bradens, would they purchase the property for them?

In an ultimate test of their commitment to the cause, the Bradens took strong, determined action by purchasing the house for the Wades. On May 15, 1954, the Wades spent the first night in their new home just two days before the landmark Supreme Court decision declaring racial segregation in schools unconstitutional. Things were looking up for a very fleeting moment—until of course the Wades' white neighbors noticed them and welcomed them to the neighborhood by burning a cross in their yard and shooting out the windows. It didn't take long for the angry neighbors to piece together that the Bradens were responsible for securing the property.

The Wade family suffered weeks of harassment and racist attacks. The Wades and Bradens organized a Wade Defense Committee, practicing community safety by ensuring someone would be available to help guard the home. Things had just started to settle down, it seemed, until, one quiet night when the Wades were fortunately away, a bomb was detonated right below two-year-old Rosemary's room, disintegrating the house they had fought so hard to make theirs.

McCarthyism was rampant at the time, and communism was the common enemy and scapegoat in the Wade case. Before the bombing, one resident wrote a letter to the editor of the *Shively Newsweek* claiming that the purchase of the home was a communist conspiracy and declaring the formation of an American White Brotherhood promoting patriotism and defense. (White supremacists! Communists! The 1950s had it all!)

Rather than focusing on finding the person or persons responsible for bombing the home of a young family, the supposed real problem to combat was communism. Investigators alleged the Bradens and their white accomplices were affiliated with the Communist Party and this alleged association somehow was the greatest threat. Racist segregationists claimed that the bombing was a communist plot to garner public attention and a fund-raising opportunity. This was never supported by anything resembling evidence.

The Bradens along with five white allies were charged with sedition because rebelling against segregation was viewed as a subversive communism act. Prosecutors portrayed Carl Braden as the leader behind the communist plot of integrated housing, and he was convicted of sedition and sentenced to fifteen years in prison. His wife and the others awaited their trials with the likelihood that a similar fate awaited them.

Having served eight months in prison, Carl was released on a $40,000 bond—at the time the highest in the commonwealth's history—after the United States Supreme Court overturned state sedition laws with its decision in *Pennsylvania v. Nelson*. The charges were dropped against the Bradens and others. The Wade family returned to a segregated neighborhood in Louisville that today remains 96 percent Black.

Amid the relief that comes with knowing they were not going to be spending the next fifteen years in prison, the Bradens returned to their lives of activism and journalism. Carl had been working as a copy editor at the *Courier Journal* since 1950, but he was fired about five minutes after his conviction. Even after his release and the dropping of charges, local employers refused to hire the Bradens, leaving them little opportunity to provide for their family.

Instead of shying away from the movement that inspired their actions, exposed them to the risk of more than a decade's imprisonment, and left them unemployed, they further embraced their convictions and took jobs as community organizers for a small civil rights organization whose mission was to turn white southerners into civil rights activists. Even though they were rejected from local media, they were able to manage their own publication with the organization's monthly newspaper, the *Southern Patriot*.

The Bradens used the years they expected to be behind bars to fully engage in civil rights advocacy. Carl died suddenly in the 1970s, and Anne carried on their shared mission, earning a collection of mugshots protesting injustice as her short bob became gray and her glasses grew thicker. Attitudes within the fight for civil rights were rapidly changing as the arc of justice was bending ever so slightly, making more progress toward racial equity. Activists, energized by this progress, became bolder in their pursuit of justice. After the civil rights victories of the 1960s, the creative extremists Dr. King described were getting more creative and extreme, inspired by some of the tactics used by the Black Panther Party.

Alberta Jones's alma mater, the segregated Louisville Municipal College (now Simmons College of Kentucky) had integrated into the University of Louisville in 1951. But by the late 1960s, the university had even fewer Black students than at the beginning of the integration. The Black Student Union had some major requests to promote racial equity on campus—development of a Pan-African Studies program, Black representation in literature through the campus library, an office on Black Affairs, hiring more Black professors (there were very few at the time), scholarships specifically for Black students, and outreach efforts in marginalized areas of Louisville.

The affable negotiations weren't completely unanswered. The university did increase the number of books in the library representing the Black experience, and they did establish some scholarships, just not nearly as many as the Black Student Union proposed. The students felt pacified, not empowered. This was a time of some progress toward the future the students wanted, but many threats to that future remained.

Racial tensions exploded in 1968 when riots broke out in Louisville in response to the assassination of Dr. King and local police brutality. Hundreds were arrested, and two Black teenagers died. Despite more diversity in housing since the Wades' home was destroyed, the idea that Black families moving into the neighborhood meant lower property values remained pervasive. After the riots, white flight was engaged like geese flying south for the winter. White business owners took their businesses out of Parkland, where the riots took place, and white residents left the West End.

While university officials and the city at large may have made the students feel merely tolerated, tactics used by activists in the Black Panther Party made them feel empowered. Instead of peacefully negotiating, the Black Panther Party presented their ten-point program as a list of demands, and they didn't request meetings to discuss their ideas. They occupied spaces where people holding power in the university sat, asserting their right to some of that power as well.

Exhausted by the lack of progress with school administrators, the University of Louisville students decided to change strategies from southern hospitality to a Black Panther–inspired occupation. They entered the university president's office and announced a takeover—time to seriously implement their demands. The best President Strickler could do was allow the students to exit the office without repercussions, which they did.

The students had occupied more than a university office. By the next day they had occupied the minds of Americans shocked that the students would escalate actions beyond just asking nicely. Members of Congress suggested investigating the protests and barring universities that tolerated such protests from securing financial aid. President Nixon suggested college administrators grow a backbone.

Meanwhile, students across the nation pressured their universities to increase Black representation, adopting some of the Black Student Union's demands of forming Pan-African Studies departments. Across the state of Kentucky, Black students were organizing and presenting their demands to universities. At the University of Kentucky, for example, the Black Student Union demanded a course in African-American history. One professor resisted, claiming a course would be too specialized and not of general interest. But hundreds of students, both white and Black, signed a petition letting the administration know they were interested. By the following year, the professor admitted he was wrong, and both the interest from the students and the civil rights developments in the country showed how necessary the course would be.

After an even more escalated occupation on the University of Louisville campus resulting in BSU activists being arrested and national pressure on the union to back down, the activists put more pressure on the university, highlighting oppression Black Kentuckians felt beyond campus. In the eyes of the student activists, the Kentucky Derby was a gleaming example of racism, as the Black community saw little of the money the most exciting two minutes in sports raked in and the Derby's Stephen Foster anthem "My Old Kentucky Home" featured some extremely problematic lyrics, including "'Tis summer, the darkies are gay."

During the Kentucky Derby of 1969, President Nixon and California governor Ronald Reagan sipped mint juleps inside Churchill Downs, while the Black Student Union picketed outside the gates. A spokesperson for the group, Blaine Hudson, prepared a statement for the demonstration criticizing President Nixon—saying he set the stage for the brutalization of Black people with his "law and order" agenda—as well as the mayor of Louisville and the Kentucky Derby legacy. The statement read:

> If people can journey across the North American continent to witness animals galloping around a

track, why is it that no one will journey across town to find living proof that Black people are not figments of an insane imagination?

If people can squander their money on questions of which animal will win a race, why is it that no one is willing to give that same amount of money to Black people—that Black people might help Black people? . . . The "darkies" are not gay any longer.

Fewer people had bet on the Black Student Union's success than the least popular Derby horse. But the demands and tactics used by the students did prove successful. By the following semester, the University of Louisville established an Office of Black Affairs and although the university didn't grant the group the proposed two hundred scholarships, twenty Black students were attending classes on scholarships that didn't exist before the students' occupation.

Other demands weren't addressed as quickly, but today the University of Louisville is a much closer reflection of the vision the Black Student Union held. By the mid-1970s the university had a Pan-African Studies program and the library had thousands of books related to the Black experience. The former spokesperson of the union who asked why so many would gamble their money in a horse race but not invest in the Black community, Blaine Hudson, became a full-time professor in the Pan-African Studies program he willed into existence. He served as the university's dean of the School of Arts and Sciences, calling the shots in an office he once occupied in the fight for racial equity.

An area of West Louisville near where the 1968 riots took place along with the exodus of white families was scouted by a developer in 2014 who had a vision of a bright new (profitable) future. The city refers to this effort as revitalization. Local activists call it gentrification. According to a lawsuit against the city of Louisville, the proposed high-end real estate development would feature new houses, a café, and an amphitheater instead of the single-family affordable housing it currently features.

The specific street, Elliott Avenue, had many vacant properties perfect for a developer to easily bulldoze and rebuild. The problem for the city and developers was the homes that were still occupied. This street became a priority for the police to investigate by late 2019. The Louisville Metro Police Department claims this effort was only a response to drive out crime. Activists claim it was an effort to drive out Black people who inconveniently have homes in an area that the city would rather see as a real estate development.

While prioritizing suspected crime on Elliott Avenue, the LMPD noticed a car that had been seen several times at a house suspected of drug activity. The police traced the car to Taylor, who lived ten miles away on the southwest side of the city. They suspected drugs were being shipped to the Elliott Avenue residence to avoid detection. A warrant was obtained and an overnight raid was planned to search the residence for any evidence of this suspected drug trafficking operation. The warrant specified that officers did not have to knock before entry "due to the nature of how these drug traffickers operate." However, before the warrant was executed, the orders were changed to knock and announce.

After midnight on March 13, 2020, LMPD officers dressed in plain clothes knocked on the apartment door listed on the warrant. During the beginning stages of the COVID-19 pandemic, most people were at home. Breonna Taylor was an essential worker enduring long shifts helping those in crisis as an emergency room technician, but she was home this late evening. At the sound of unexpected banging on her door, according to her boyfriend Kenneth Walker, she asked, "Who is it?"

No response.

According to Walker, she asked several more times. No answer. At this time, he decided to arm himself, believing that intruders were breaking into the apartment. He fired what he called a "warning shot," hoping to scare away the intruders and prevent any danger to himself or Breonna as the police deployed a battering ram to force entry. Then the police fired thirty-two shots into the apartment. Five of the bullets hit Breonna, killing her. No drugs or evidence of a drug trafficking operation were discovered at the scene.

On Memorial Day, an intimate service took place outside Breonna's apartment to honor her memory and call for justice. Breonna's family, Black Lives Matter Louisville organizers, and Until Freedom activist Tamika Mallory gathered to lay a wreath in front of the apartment building still riddled with bullet holes. The crowd paying their respects to Breonna was small enough to gather in the narrow parking lot.

That evening in Minneapolis, a forty-six-year-old Black man, George Floyd, was killed after a police officer subdued him by kneeling on his neck for more than eight minutes. Later that week, many cities across the country, including Louisville, erupted in protests. Hundreds demonstrated to demand justice for Breonna and George with chants of "No justice, no peace, prosecute the police!" and "Say her name—BREONNA TAYLOR!" echoing through the downtown Louisville streets.

In July, the New York–based social justice group Until Freedom, which had organized the small-scale memorial for Breonna at her apartment in May, kept returning to Louisville and bringing attention to Breonna's case with large demonstrations. They organized buses to bring protestors from Louisville to the state capital in Frankfort and demand the Kentucky attorney general, Daniel Cameron, charge the officers involved, now that he was in charge of the investigation. The demonstration, with hundreds of protestors, media coverage, and celebrities, ensured that the commonwealth and the world heard Breonna Taylor's name. But the group wasn't feeling heard by Cameron.

Say her name—BREONNA TAYLOR!

So in July the group mobilized protestors and rented more buses. They conducted a direct action training, explaining that the possibility of arrest at this action was high, and how to act if arrested to prevent further harm. The large group of protestors hopped on the chartered buses with the phone number for legal defense written on their arms and no idea where the bus was headed or what exactly the direct action was.

After a confusing drive across town and a march through a residential street, the group had finally arrived at their destination—Attorney General Cameron's home. The group, including an attorney, a reality TV star, an NFL wide receiver, a pastor, and dozens of local activists, occupied the lawn chanting, "You can't stop the revolution!" One by one, all eighty-seven left the freshly manicured lawn in handcuffs.

By August, LMPD had arrested five hundred protestors over seventy-five days of protests and spent millions in overtime as local activists called for divesting money from the police and investing that money into the Black community.

After the daily protests—including one organized outside Churchill Downs during the Kentucky Derby—and subsequent arrests, local bail funds worked to release arrested protestors as quickly as possible. Jefferson Square Park sits near the jail where protestors are arrested and released as well as the county courthouse.

Protestors launched an occupation of the park and renamed it Injustice Square. For more than a year after her death, art, letters, flowers, and signs were displayed as a memorial to Breonna with a painting of her smiling image standing in the center.

Throughout the months of protests, the square has not been as idyllic as it often appears. One night after a right-wing militia threatened to restore order in the area and tensions were especially high, a young photographer, Tyler Gerth, was killed in the square as an unintended victim in a dispute. The square has often been the setting for arrests and confrontations with the police where protestors have been hit with rubber bullets, flashbangs, and tear gas.

Still, most days before the sun set and the threat of conflict heightened, the square appeared to be quite the racially just utopia it strived to be. Local community groups that had long established themselves would arrive at the square just the way some arrive at the office in the morning because this is their work. They spent their days providing protestors and other residents with information about bail support, voting, and community resources, and they would even serve meals. Rogue gardeners planted a community garden in the green spaces around Breonna's memorial, and when the garden produced fresh veggies, they donated them to those in the West End most affected by the lack of accessible food.

In 1973 civil rights activist Angela Davis had the vision to form a national organizing collective committed to freeing activists of color from jail, and she asked her friend Carl Braden to help turn this vision into reality. Soon the Kentucky Alliance Against Racist and Political Repression was formed in Louisville, committed to combatting police brutality and economic inequality and to teaching others about institutionalized racism and how it affects our lives and communities. Still active today, the Kentucky Alliance Against Racist and Political Repression holds press conferences at the Carl Braden Memorial House in the West End, and during the protests it regularly engaged with the community at Injustice Square.

Antiracism was at the core of the Alliance's structure. It was made clear that white and Black activists would be sharing power and that white people should be comfortable with Black folks taking the lead on organizing, especially in matters of racial justice. Shameka Parrish-Wright has been involved with the Alliance since the early 2000s when she began as an intern and Anne Braden gave her a box of reading material, instructing her to read up on the mission of the Alliance.

Even years after Anne's death, a large puppet version of her featuring her gray bob and thick glasses accompanies the Alliance to protests. In an interview with the Anne Braden Institute for Social Justice Research, Shameka said of Anne:

"When I first met her, I was just so impressed that this old white woman was working on issues of racism, just tirelessly. I knew I wanted to help her in whatever she was doing. I was like, dang! If she's doing all that, the least I can do is help."

During the daily protests of 2020, Shameka spent her days at the square, bailing out protestors and continuing to spread the mission taught to her by Anne, who once said:

"In every age, no matter how cruel the oppression carried on by those in power, there have been those who struggled for a different world. I believe this is the genius of humankind, the thing that makes us half divine; the fact that some human beings can envision a world that has never existed."

Fight for a Racially Just Kentucky

- Realize your potential like Alberta. Take inventory of the unique gifts and talents you bring to social justice work. Contribute to the fight for racial justice by using your strengths. For example, if you're great at organization and have a great eye for detail, consider the logistic side, such as bail support, or maintain databases of volunteers with local organizations. Think about how you can best serve the community in the pursuit of racial equity.

- Learn to make space like Anne. The Bradens understood how vital the practice of antiracism is to combatting injustice and knew it was their responsibility, as white allies, to fight systemic racism. Practice antiracism in your daily life, and if you're a white ally, step aside for Black organizers to lead. Listen to how you can best support, but don't take over.

- Be bold like Blaine. He stood strong in his convictions, and when he sensed it was time to escalate, he pushed forward. Be willing to step outside your comfort zone and take risks. But never be careless; be strategic and keep the goal in mind.

- Help like Breonna. She dedicated her career to helping others in their worst days, saving gunshot victims, and treating medical crises. Her friends described her as kind, funny, and vivacious. Through her training as an EMT, she picked up on medical jargon and terms that she applied to situations beyond the emergency room. One of these phrases was "Apply the pressure!" As her friends and family gathered outside the statehouse in Frankfort along with hundreds of others demanding action, they chanted it back and forth to each other—"Apply the pressure!"—and responded with "Pressure applied!"

- Be like Breonna. Apply the pressure.

SEVEN

LGBTQ+ RIGHTS

THIS LOVE STORY is not the exciting tale that Nicholas Sparks might dream up or that would inspire a romantic comedy with a script irresistible to Rachel McAdams. Even the people involved in this story admit that their family is, well, just as boring and ordinary as any other family. Like most how-we-met stories, it includes a lovely couple who are very much in love, and like most how-we-met stories, you've probably heard it all before. Here it goes.

The couple met at a bar. They were instantly smitten—love at first sight, if you will. Months after the first meeting, they moved in together, unable to stand to be apart any longer. They knew they wanted to have children, and soon they had three. They lived happily ever after . . .

. . . with a few hiccups along the way.

The couple in this story, Paul Campion and Randy Johnson, instantly fell for each other and wanted to spend their lives together, be a family, and frankly just have an ordinary, boring life like everyone else's in which a couple is fortunate enough to grow old together, still as in love as the day they met. But they had to make a pit stop at the United States Supreme Court to make that dream a reality.

Although Paul was born and raised in Jamestown, New York, and Randy near Louisville, they shared the extremely difficult experience for young gay men of living in conservative towns and being born to religious families. Paul had tried to reject his sexuality until he met Randy and could no longer deny who it was he was meant to love.

The couple shared strong values and a deep desire to have children and to be a family. As they began their adoption search in 1994, they were successful with only one agency that would allow a gay man to adopt a child.

This particular agency, Adoptions of Kentucky, had the radical view that whether or not someone would be a good parent was more important than stereotypes and prejudice. (Now imagine Meryl Streep's character in *The Devil Wears Prada* sarcastically saying, "Groundbreaking.") What a surprise—it was determined that these two men would be great parents.

But, in what would become one of their early legal hindrances, only one of them could be named the legal guardian of the child. Undeterred, Paul was named the guardian of their first two children, Tevin and Tyler (twins!), who were born in 1995. They later added to their family with a daughter, Mackenzie, born in 2003. This time Randy was named the legal guardian. In 2006, Paul was working in education and met eight-year-old DeSean, whom they also adopted.

Parenthood was challenging enough without the worry of legal guardianship issues hanging over their heads. But the couple had concerns about what might happen if one parent died and the other parent didn't have legal guardianship over all of their children. After Proposition 8 passed, the couple took the opportunity to marry in California. They were visiting Paul's brother in Palm Springs, and when he reminded the couple that they could legally get married now, they jumped on it as quickly as a Las Vegas elopement. But Kentucky, where they lived, didn't legally recognize their union.

In 2013, after twenty-three years of being together, they spotted an intriguing post while they scrolled the newsfeed. A friend shared that some local lawyers were looking for same-sex couples to join a lawsuit challenging the existing ban on same-sex marriages.

The couple had never thought of themselves as activists, but they wanted to deepen their connection to the LGBTQ+ community. And of course the ultimate goal was to have their marriage recognized at home, to finally be legally recognized as the family they had been for so long.

The previous year, the "in sickness and in health" portion of their vows was tested when Paul was diagnosed with prostate cancer at age forty-six. So not only did they have to deal with a heavy load of worry and decide on a treatment plan. They also suddenly had to figure out the legal issues, beginning with whether Randy would be recognized by medical providers as Paul's husband.

"I am healthy now and cancer free," Paul said recently. "However, at the time we were very concerned for several reasons. First, we were worried about the most appropriate treatment and navigating through the options that would be best for me. Secondly, Randy was not legally related to me at the time because Kentucky would not recognize our marriage from California. Therefore, doctors and the medical industry did not have to legally recognize him, which concerned us greatly. We had to shop for providers that would recognize Randy as my husband. The most worrisome part of having cancer was the concern of the possibility of not surviving. Randy had no legal connection to the three boys, and if I had passed away, my parents had more legal rights than Randy did. He also wouldn't receive any survivor benefits."

They first asked their kids about the possibility of joining a marriage equality lawsuit, and the kids quickly gave their blessing. The couple decided to join other plaintiffs, many of whom had been together for decades also, in the Kentucky marriage cases *Bourke v. Beshear* and *Love v. Beshear*.

Historically, Kentucky has played a big role in influencing LGBTQ+ laws in and beyond the commonwealth. In 1986 a twenty-three-year-old nursing student, Jeffrey Wasson, was arrested and charged with solicitation of same-sex sodomy. Apparently, in the mid-1980s, police thought consensual sex between two men that affects no one else was, for some reason, a big threat. So they organized sting operations to catch them.

When Wasson left a gay bar in Lexington, an undercover officer approached him and taped twenty minutes of a flirty conversation. The officer asked for more details about what they might do later. He suggested that they go to his place and have some totally consensual sex that happened to violate a 1974 statute banning the act. Just a regular ol' hookup after a night of drinks that would have ended much differently had an undercover cop not been involved.

Instead of paying the fine, Wasson decided to fight the law. First, he won! The judge at Fayette District Court dismissed the charges because, duh. More specifically, he said that the law was unconstitutional. But of course things did not end there, as the commonwealth was quite stubborn. On appeal, the Fayette Circuit Court agreed with the District Court decision—another win for Wasson. Then the commonwealth appealed again, and the case went to the Kentucky Supreme Court.

In 1992, after years of Wasson being uplifted by a victory and then dejected by facing yet another appeal, the Kentucky Supreme Court narrowly struck down antisodomy laws that had been in effect since 1860. As previous courts had declared, the state's high court agreed these laws were unconstitutional, violating the right to privacy and the right to equal protection under the law.

Wasson's victory was one of the early wins striking down discriminatory laws involving consensual sex between men. Several cases in other states successfully cited the Kentucky case to strike down their own discriminatory laws. But as states struck down these laws, federal law still criminalized homosexual sodomy. Eventually, thanks in part to the precedent set in the Kentucky case, federal sodomy laws were finally struck down with the United States Supreme Court case *Lawrence v. Texas* in 2003.

Just more than two decades after Wasson's victory, another major case seeking civil rights for LGBTQ+ Kentuckians was headed to the United States Supreme Court. *Obergefell v. Hodges* was not just one case representing one couple, it was a super case consolidating six lower-court cases and sixteen same-sex couples from Ohio, Michigan, Tennessee, and Kentucky.

Six Kentucky couples were among the plaintiffs:

- Paul Campion and Randy Johnson, the couple with the typical love story, had been together for twenty-five years at the time and had four children.

- Gregory Bourke and Michael DeLeon, a couple from Louisville, had been together since 1981 and had two children. Like Campion and Johnson, they also had split legal guardship of their children.
- Kim Franklin and Tammy Boyd had been together eight years and had married in 2010 on the beach in Connecticut, an occasion Franklin referred to as the day she felt all her dreams were coming true.
- Jim Meade and Luke Barlowe had been together for forty-six years, having first met at a Louisville bar in 1968. Also, like Campion and Johnson, they shared the scary experience of battling a cancer diagnosis, non-Hodgkin's lymphoma, and the legal challenges of not having the same rights and security other married couples have.
- Timothy Love and Larry Ysunza had been together thirty-four years and had a civil union ceremony in Vermont in 2000. But they chose to wait to marry until they legally could in Kentucky, where they live. They also suffered health scares and discriminatory legal complications when Love was hospitalized and sent for emergency surgery after two blockages were found in his heart. Amid the scare, Ysunza had to quickly complete legal paperwork allowing him to

make healthcare decisions for Love had he become incapacitated.

- Dominique James and Reverend Maurice "Bojangles" Blanchard had been together since 2004 and married in a religious ceremony in 2006, which was meaningful to the deeply spiritual couple. They attempted to get a marriage license and were denied in 2013. After the denial, according to the American Civil Liberties Union of Kentucky, Reverend Blanchard said, "We can no longer be silent accomplices to our own discrimination." And so they were not.

Attorney Dan Canon represented Timothy Love and Larry Ysunza. He explained a bit about the legal strategy and what brought them to the United States Supreme Court, an experience he simply describes as "wild as hell."

"The Kentucky case happened in two phases," said Dan. "After the decision in the *United States v. Windsor*, the national sentiment was that we'd have a decent shot at convincing the lower courts that states had to recognize valid marriages from other states. So we sued on behalf of couples who were married in Iowa and Connecticut, where it was already legal, to get their marriages recognized by Kentucky.

"When we won the 'recognition' phase, Tim Love and Larry Ysunza came to us and said, 'We've been together for thirty years in Kentucky and we'd like to get married in our home state.' The court had already basically told us that it would rule in our favor in a 'licensure' case, so to make a long story short, we added Tim and Larry to the existing lawsuit."

It was a common complaint for couples to experience the terror of an unexpected health crisis while not having the legal right to make decisions on behalf of, or simply be with, the person you love and have committed your life to. But outside of the logistics, for many like Dan, fighting for the right of these couples to marry was just the right thing to do.

I don't think the importance is so much legal as it is moral.
—Dan Canon

"I don't think the importance is so much legal as it is moral," said Dan. "Tim and Larry, like the rest of our Kentucky clients, are firmly rooted in Kentucky; it's where their friends and family live, it's where they work, it's where they go to school and church, it's *home*. Why should they have to go somewhere else to get married? The very idea that someone should have to travel to another state, or even another county, to marry someone they've lived with for decades is a big part of what's so offensive to the concept of 'equal dignity' that Justice Kennedy writes about in the Obergefell opinion."

Justice Anthony Kennedy, a Reagan appointee and a conservative, recognized the rights and liberty of LGBTQ+ Americans in several landmark cases, serving as the swing vote in 5–4 decisions. In *Romer v. Evans*, the court struck down discrimination based on sexual orientation. In *Lawrence v. Texas* (remember Wasson's case in Kentucky?), same-sex sex acts were no longer criminalized. In *Obergefell v. Hodges*, constitutional protection was granted to same-sex couples.

Here's the final paragraph of Justice Kennedy's opinion in *Obergefell v. Hodges*:

No union is more profound than marriage, for it embodies the highest ideals of love, fidelity, devotion, sacrifice, and family. In forming a marital union, two people become something greater than once they were. As some of the petitioners in these cases demonstrate, marriage embodies a love that may endure even past death. It would misunderstand these men and women to say they disrespect the idea of marriage. Their plea is that they do respect it, respect it so deeply that they seek to find its fulfillment for themselves. Their hope is not to be condemned to live in loneliness, excluded from one of civilization's oldest institutions. They ask for equal dignity in the eyes of the law. The Constitution grants them that right.

I mean, who knew that SCOTUS could be so romantic?

When the Supreme Court ruled in favor of the plaintiffs, discriminatory laws banning same-sex marriage were struck down and marriage equality became the law of the land in all fifty states. Crowds waving rainbow flags celebrated not only outside the SCOTUS building but all across the nation. The White House was illuminated in a rainbow, showing support for the ruling.

Many couples named in the cases were seen holding their loved one's hands over their heads and cheering. Jim Obergefell, the primary plaintiff named in the case, had not a hand to hold. What many of the plaintiffs had feared, and worked so hard to prevent, had already happened to Obergefell. He entered accidental activism upon the death of his husband of twenty-two years, John Arthur, in 2013. After Arthur's death, Obergefell was unable to be legally recognized as his surviving spouse on the death certificate.

When marriage equality reached Kentucky, not everyone celebrated. The commonwealth didn't have a very strong history of being warm to same-sex couples and their right to be legally recognized.

In 1973, the Kentucky Court of Appeals ruled in *Jones v. Hallahan* that the two women seeking a marriage license were properly denied. But they didn't even try very hard to come up with a good excuse. The commonwealth at this time did not restrict marriage to heterosexual couples. So the court cited the dictionary definition of marriage and simply ruled that "the relationship proposed is not a marriage." It was like the judicial version of your mom running out of reasons and just saying, "Because I said so."

In 1998, Kentucky legislators came up with their definition of marriage so they no longer had to refer to Merriam-Webster. They defined marriage as a relationship between a man and a woman. They also prohibited same-sex marriage from taking place within the commonwealth, and they refused to recognize same-sex marriages from any other jurisdiction.

In 2004, Kentucky voters got their say on the issue when a constitutional amendment was proposed, it read:

Only a marriage between one man and one woman shall be valid or recognized as a marriage in Kentucky. A legal status identical or substantially similar to that of marriage for unmarried individuals shall not be valid or recognized.

The marriage equality ban easily passed, with 75 percent of voters in favor of the amendment, which—considering 2004 wasn't all that long ago—paints quite a grim picture of recent public opinion surrounding LGBTQ+ rights in Kentucky.

Rowan County Clerk Kim Davis received national notoriety after refusing to do her job and issue marriage licenses to same-sex couples after the Obergefell decision. Davis had personally been married four times to three different husbands. Her second husband is also her husband in her fourth marriage and the adoptive father of twins fathered by the third husband while she was married to the first. There's a couple of other kids too. Did you follow that? I had to make a chart. Anyway, the point is, Davis claimed she had strong personal beliefs about the sanctity of marriage based on her religious beliefs, and darn it, only men and women are allowed to marry and divorce as many times as they'd like.

"I think the sharp backlash to sudden progress is inevitable, " said Dan Canon, " and that should be apparent to anyone who's looked at the history of social movements in the U.S. The good news is: it's hard to un-ring the human rights bell once it's been rung. While I'm distressed by the extent to which the courts, and the general public, have accepted discriminatory treatment of LGBTQ+ folks as 'religious freedom,' even the most powerful bigots have been thus far unsuccessful at turning back the clock."

Kim Davis had support from conservative leaders such as Mike Huckabee, but although he posed for some pictures, he and other high-profile conservatives left Kentucky and, well, that was about it. She asked for help, demanding to be exempt from issuing marriage licenses to couples she personally did not believe should be married. The county clerk's name appeared on marriage licenses, and she did not want her name on the license of a same-sex couple because, if it's not clear by now, she didn't like it. Supreme Court be damned, she just didn't like it. But everyone pretty much reminded her she had no choice, this was the law, and she also took an oath of office to do this job.

Given a federal judge's order to issue marriage licenses to same-sex couples, Davis continued to deny them. So she was held in contempt and went to jail for five days. A legal battle ensued, with the ACLU defending the position of same-sex couples fighting for their legal right to be married. Davis's hissy fit resulted in the removal of the clerk's name from the licenses.

Then gubernatorial candidate Matt Bevin gave Davis his strong support as she denied licenses and then was named in the related court challenges. After Bevin won the election and a court ordered the state of Kentucky— and thus its taxpayers—to pay more than $222,000 in legal fees incurred by the same-sex couples who sued, Governor Bevin's support wavered, and he said she broke the law and she, not Kentucky, must pay. His attorney, Palmer G. Vance II, said, "Only Davis refused to comply with the law as was her obligation and as required by the oath of office she took." In the end, even Bevin took the "Come on, lady, you had one job" approach.

Davis attempted to take her case to the Supreme Court of the United States, but they declined. She lost her reelection bid and the job she refused to do in 2018.

"From what I've heard from clients," said Canon, "things were obviously very bad on a macrocosmic level before *Obergefell*, and it's not like marriage equality somehow made everything better. But on a microcosmic, person-to-person level, it's interesting to note that a lot of our clients were more accepted than one might think by their neighbors, and sometimes even their broader communities—even in rural areas. There is this sentiment that 'being gay is not okay, but you're different because we know you and *you're* okay.' Cases like *Obergefell* are important because they mark an institutional seal of approval on a type of relationship, and by extension a type of person. In other words, if a court says 'you're okay,' it removes some of the fear of the unknown, making it easier for the rest of society to say 'you're okay,' whether they know you or not.

"As far as the work left to do, there's a lot. Now that the LGBTQ+ community has gained more mainstream acceptance, 'T' has become the main lightning rod. State legislatures are introducing wantonly cruel anti-trans bills every session. I think it's only a matter of time before these controversies over bathrooms and sports become silly relics of the past, but in the meantime lots of people—especially kids—are going to be hurt very badly, I'm afraid."

Paul Campion agrees that while Kentucky has made some progress toward LGBTQ+ equality, there's still work to be done. He sees Jefferson County as being quite progressive and warm to the LGBTQ+ community, but not so much across the rest of the commonwealth. That's why he supports a statewide Fairness Ordinance to protect all Kentuckians in the LGBTQ+ community.

After the Obergefell decision, Paul and Randy were able to finally be recognized legally as the family they had been for so long. They adopted each other's children, which they were parenting together, and they were granted all the benefits any married couple is granted. The twins they brought home as infants, Tevin and Tyler, are now college graduates and growing their careers. DeSean is working and in a happy relationship. The baby, Mackenzie, has plans to attend nursing school. Paul and Randy just celebrated their thirtieth anniversary of being together and loving each other.

Sisterly Love

No one attending a bachelorette party at a gay bar or a parade celebrating LGBTQ+ pride could possibly miss the presence of the Sisters of Perpetual Indulgence. They're often spotted passing out condoms to promote safer sex, making snarky jokes, dancing, and taking photos. Their appearance could best be described as nuns . . . in drag. They wear habits, lots of accessories, full-face makeup, and daintily hold their flowing skirts as they move around the room angelically. They're mesmerizing.

The Derby City Sisters, a Kentucky chapter of the Sisters of Perpetual Indulgence, are a fixture in LGBTQ+ advocacy. They're not just a social club, they're an operating charity which contributes to many other local charities. They host tons of fund-raising events, and they donate items to those in need, such as the unhoused.

They describe themselves as queer nuns and officially state, "Our outrageous finery is a reminder that if there is a place for a bunch of wacky drag nuns, there is a place for you. You can find us at bars, festivals, bingo halls, and your local street corner. Basically, anywhere in need of some joy."

One regular event they host, a bingo night at Louisville's premier gay bar, Play, benefits a different local charity every month. This event is so much fun, it's actually turned into a regular date night activity for my husband and me. We never seem to win, but we spend a couple of hours laughing until our cheeks hurt and knowing the money we have spent is going to a worthy cause. The atmosphere the Sisters create is positive, welcoming, and infectious. If you're in a bad mood when you enter, they'll shake it out of you.

"I joined the Sisters for a new social group and because I like to do charity work," said Sister Petty Davis. "But it turned out that when I learned more about our core missions, which are to spread joy and expiate stigmatic guilt, I realized that to fulfill those vows, I needed to find more joy in my own life.

"I started looking for things that make me joyful, and openly acknowledging them. This didn't just make me a better Sister. It improved my life drastically. Manifesting joy in my life made me so much happier, and able to spread joy. That is what I love most about being a Sister."

Their outfits and demeanors may make you laugh, but the vows Sisters take are serious. Among other requirements, each new member must take on a novice project before becoming a fully professed Sister. When Sister Petty Davis joined, she created a fund-raiser selling prayer candles with portraits of the Sisters. I'm the proud owner of a candle featuring Sister Slut Muffin, which I adore so much I've never lit it. Sister Petty Davis raised $4,500 selling the candles, and the funds went to a new shelter for LGBTQ+ youth, Sweet Evening Breeze.

Outside of charity work, the Sisters also advocate for LGBTQ+-friendly policies. They even met Governor Andy Beshear, much to the chagrin of irritable homophobes. But Sister Petty Davis points that the energy they exude—that electric positive energy that feels like a glittery hug—is intentional. Their main mission is spreading joy, and that matters too.

"At the Kentuckiana Pride Festival, I was walking around and met a nice lady who was running a face painting booth for kids," said Sister Davis. "She asked me if I would help her out on her eyelashes, and so I did. I always carry lipstick and lash glue in my purse! As I was putting on her lashes, she told me how her child had been a drag queen and had said he wanted her to wear big lashes, but he passed before he taught her how. Well, obviously, I'm about to cry at this point, but I got the lashes on her, and she hugged me and thanked me for bringing her a little of him back. It is so magical to me that the act of dressing up like a glamorous fool opens people up to you. People share joys and pain with us all the time, and it is really beautiful."

Protect LGBTQ+ Rights and Spread Joy

- Learn from the lived experiences of "accidental activists" who bravely fight for their rights, like Paul Campion and his husband Randy Johnson, and recognize their contributions to the landmark civil rights battle.
- Take Dan Canon's example of recognizing the right time to do the right thing. The legal strategy was focused and strategic. But the motive behind it was to recognize the civil rights of the LGBTQ+ because it's what they deserve.
- Treat civil rights and dignity as a moral issue, not necessarily a political one. Discrimination should never be part of a political platform, and everyone should stand in opposition to discrimination against the LGBTQ+ community.
- Pay special attention, as Canon said, to the "T" portion of LGBTQ+, people who face the brunt of current discriminatory policies affecting the

community. Support local groups who support trans Kentuckians.

- Spread joy like the Derby City Sisters. You don't have to wear a habit or learn how to properly apply false lashes. Try to re-create that positive energy that allows everyone to embrace their authentic selves.

EIGHT

IMMIGRATION

DURING HIS CAMPAIGN for president, Donald Trump called for a deportation force to deport all migrants living in the United States illegally. He parroted cruel stereotypes and hurled insults at Hispanic immigrants, suggesting that Mexicans bring crime and drugs across the border to the United States and calling them rapists. He vowed to rescind Obama's actions on Deferred Action for Childhood Arrivals (DACA) and Deferred Action for Parents of U.S. Citizens and Lawful Permanent Residents (DAPA). He proposed a ban on Muslims entering, saying

separated from their families. Hundreds of families are still separated, and immigration activists are desperately trying to complete the complicated task of reuniting them.

Although President Trump touted the plan as removing dangerous criminals from our communities and either putting them in prison or sending them back to their countries for imprisonment, most of the migrant families targeted did not have criminal histories. Many of those affected were just families looking for a better life, who thought they had found one here.

As the raids conducted by Immigration and Customs Enforcement (ICE) began, with the threat of more happening, immigrants lived in terrified anticipation of being uprooted, separated from their families, and sent back to places they no longer considered home.

As this news hit Louisville, dozens of members of the immigration rights group Mijente Louisville as well as the racial justice groups Black Lives Matter Louisville and Louisville Standing Up for Racial Justice gathered their camping gear. They set up camp at 6 a.m. Monday morning outside the ICE office in downtown Louisville, with no plans to leave. They occupied the space to call attention to the mass deportations and Kentucky's compliance in assisting with them. They believed this immigration issue was a human rights issue and the best way to address it was to bring in other people who were not directly affected but who were disgusted with ICE's actions and desperate to do something, anything, about it.

Mijente Louisville leader Jesús Ibáñez told the Louisville news station WHAS 11, "The point is not to feel comfortable. The point of the protests is to feel the uncomfortableness that people being persecuted feel daily. So yes, we are here to make people feel uncomfortable."

Jesús's hometown of San Jose, California, boasts a vibrant immigrant community with nearly 40 percent of the population born outside the United States. Like so many other Californians, his parents were born south of the border in a small Mexican town. After he took the Law School Admission Test, Jesús vowed to attend the first law school that accepted him. The University of Louisville Brandeis School of Law beat the University of San Francisco in sending Jesús an acceptance and determined the fate of his legal education.

Jesús seems quite comfortable making others uncomfortable in order to draw attention to dire issues. He earned his Juris Doctor just months before occupying the ICE offices. On the commencement stage, his brightly colored serape symbolizing his heritage contrasted with the black robes and white people surrounding him. A graduate behind him is pictured giving his best Jim Halpert impression with a tightly closed smirk. Jesús stands stoically, facing forward, holding a sign that reads "DISMANTLE I.C.E. CHINGA LA MIGRA."

We've had one Yiddish swearing lesson in this book so far, and now it's time for a Spanish one. "Chinga la Migra" means "fuck Immigration," referring to those in positions of power to detain and deport immigrants. It has referred to the Border Patrol and specifically, in this case, to ICE.

The activism of Mijente Louisville isn't just bold—it's spicy. Serrano pepper spicy. Ghost pepper spicy. When the Mijente members arrived at the ICE office, they wasted no time and barricaded the only entry and exit to the agency's parking lot, so detainee transport vans couldn't be used. They got comfortable in their pursuit of making others uncomfortable and set up approximately twenty tents on the grounds in front of the office.

Unfortunately for the activists, taking on the Department of Homeland Security and occupying federal property proved to be no easy feat. They were kicked off the premises, though they remained on the sidewalk, considered public property, to continue protests. As agents destroyed the barricade and several tents, activists yelled at them from a distance, "Gestapo!"

The activists named their sidewalk occupation and row of tents Camp Compasión and refused to vacate. After more than two weeks of protests and refusals to comply with Louisville Metro Police Department's numerous requests to leave the public property surrounding the ICE office, Mayor Greg Fischer released a statement on Twitter announcing the city's next steps:

> In communities across our nation, including here in Louisville, Americans are demanding that Washington finally overhaul our immigration laws to ensure safe borders, a path to citizenship for Dreamers, & to reform ICE so that immigrants & refugees are treated fairly & humanely.
>
> Our city welcomes immigrants and strongly opposes the separation of families.
>
> We also strongly support the right of protesters to exercise the First Amendment, which includes the right to peacefully assemble. While exercising that right, protestors must also follow the law.

This morning, after multiple unsuccessful requests to the protesters, LMPD brought protesters outside the federal Immigrations and Customs Office into compliance with state and federal laws.

According to the Mijente activists, being "put into compliance" meant they were startled awake in the wee hours of the morning by LMPD officers in riot gear who quickly threw supplies—tents, coolers, food, clothing—into a large dump truck headed for the property room. Nearby a van large enough for mass arrests stood idle. Although Camp Compasión was quickly demolished, the group vowed not to let the eviction destroy their conviction.

In a statement released by Mijente on Facebook, Jesús summarized the LMPD actions, then said:

LMPD distributed flyers stating the raid was to "seize property considered abandoned," which is ridiculous. If the property was abandoned, why was it necessary for police to come decked out in riot gear with an arrest wagon? Why come prepared for a riot? Abandoned items can not fight back, and there were less than 20 sleeping campers onsite when the raid began. . . .

The so-called Compassionate City of Louisville and Mayor Fischer have made it very clear they do not care about the treatment of our immigrant community, by deliberately turning a blind eye to horrors being perpetrated by ICE and the unlawful behavior of LMPD. Instead, they choose to antagonize those who act to disrupt it. They pretend to fret about ADA regulations and "public safety," while Camp Compasión stood peacefully as a model of radical love, hospitality, and resistance for all who built community with us.

The heavy-handed tactics used by the city and LMPD have only served to strengthen our resolve. We will be as defiant as ever. Our mission is still to #AbolishICE in order to #FreeOurFuture; we will not falter.

Chinga La Migra.

Bearing Witness

Survivor of the Auschwitz and Buchenwald concentration camps during the Holocaust, Elie Wiesel spent the remainder of his eighty-seven years on Earth sharing the atrocities he had endured, in a relentless effort to ensure that such unfathomable cruelty could never happen again. He wrote fifty-seven books, most of which were nonfiction works and literature about the Holocaust. He offered many thoughts about what tools best combat hate and about the endurance of the human spirit.

Yet on the subject of how the Holocaust happened and how any human could be so callous as to participate in it, he offered no theories. In his intimate knowledge of the events, he confirmed what you may suspect—it's beyond comprehension. But while he couldn't explain why it happened, he knew that it did, and he offered his experience as a witness so others might draw their own lessons from it.

Wiesel once said that the opposite of love is not hate but indifference. Eleven months spent imprisoned in a concentration camp enduring torture and witnessing ruthless brutality gave him much opportunity to contemplate the role indifference played.

And what is memory if not a noble and necessary response to and against indifference?
—Elie Wiesel

In a speech to the United Nations titled "Bearing Witness, 60 Years On," Wiesel spoke of the duty and power a witness carries:

> And now, years later, you who represent the entire world community, listen to the words of the witness. . . .
>
> The Jewish witness speaks of his people's suffering as a warning. He sounds the alarm so as to prevent these things being done. . . .
>
> Those who survived Auschwitz advocate hope, not despair; generosity, not rancor or bitterness; gratitude, not violence. We must be engaged, we must reject indifference as an option. Indifference always helps the aggressor, never his victims. And what is memory if not a noble and necessary response to and against indifference?
>
> But . . . will the world ever learn?

When the cruelty along the border was exposed, much of the Jewish community heard the call to bear witness and see with their own eyes what migrants were experiencing there. One of many Jewish groups to travel to the border was the Jewish Council for Public Affairs delegation with twenty-three members across twelve states representing local Jewish Community Relations Councils and other Jewish agencies. These members included rabbis, community leaders, and Kentuckian Beth Salamon.

"As a Jew, I was horrified," said Beth. "When you met these families and you heard about why they were fleeing, and what they were facing in their countries, it was just horrifying."

As an attorney, Beth has the skills to navigate convoluted scenarios and translate legalese with ease. But at the border she witnessed families trapped in legal limbo. They came to the United States to seek asylum after fleeing dire circumstances in their home countries. If they didn't starve in the midst of mass food insecurity, they might fall victim to gang violence. For the migrants, fighting for their lives meant surrendering everything they had—their homes, their cultures, family ties, their businesses—in order to flee for the United States.

Beth was shocked to learn about strange legal loopholes she was never taught in law school or came across in practice. For example, the Fourth Amendment to the U.S. Constitution protects people from random and unnecessary stops and searches without a warrant. But the federal government claims that doesn't apply within one hundred miles of a border. No, really. Google it.

The process of seeking asylum is well established in international law, dating back to provisions in the Geneva Convention after World War II as a direct response to persecution of Jews and other groups targeted by the Nazi Party. It has been used in the United States since 1980. Asylum serves as a form of protection and is granted to those who cannot return to their home country because of persecution or reasonable fear of persecution due to their race, religion, nationality, membership in a particular social group, or political stance. So, based on this, someone fleeing rampant gang violence in Honduras, for example, would meet this basic criterion, right? Right.

In between chants of "Build the wall," Donald Trump warned that drug dealers and rapists were hopping the border to take our jobs. (Perhaps drug dealing isn't as lucrative as once thought?) But many migrants affected by Trump's zero tolerance policy were following a well established legal process of seeking asylum. The process for legally seeking asylum seems fairly straightforward:

Step one: Go to the United States. This is usually the hard part. If you're in an impossible situation in your home country with death looming, you likely meet the criteria for seeking asylum. But there isn't a process for applying in advance. There's no form to fill out, no one you can email, no visa available. You must physically get to the United States.

Step two: State your intention to seek asylum and support the request with evidence. You cannot arrive in the United States and seek asylum because you heard mint juleps are tasty (a lie) and decided to take root in the Bluegrass. You must meet the criteria, which likely means you are in a desperate situation in which your home country represents death and the United States represents life.

That's it, just two steps. Going to the border and seeking asylum is not only legal to do, it's the only way you *can* legally seek asylum. But the process became especially murky during the Trump administration. A migrant family might arrive at the border with only one thing—each other—but at the border they were forcibly separated. Afterwards they were challenged to unweave a tangled web of immigration court proceedings. Members of the same family didn't necessarily meet the same fate: one might be granted asylum and one deported. At the time of this writing, hundreds of children remain separated from their families with little hope of reunification.

"It's very complicated," said Beth. "Even after seventy-two hours of trying to figure out the system, my head was swimming. It's such a mess. I don't understand how anybody could navigate it. The people we met were trying to cross legally through the asylum system, but at the same time, Trump kept moving the goalposts. At first they were denying asylum claims to almost everybody. Then they insinuated that you have to request asylum in the countries that you cross through before you could request in America. So you meet these people in the shelter and they're waiting their turn, and we just all know that they're going to be sent back to their countries. They're not going to be successful because nobody was successful."

If an American attorney has a difficult time navigating the system, you can imagine how difficult it could be for a migrant whose native language isn't English or who may not speak English at all. Migrants with legal representation fare better in the courts, but it's tricky to snag an immigration attorney with such high demand. The migrants did everything they could to follow the rules, but the rules suddenly changed.

In order to better understand the border crisis and properly advocate for solid immigration policies, the delegation Beth traveled with visited a variety of people who work along the border daily. This included volunteers for humanitarian organizations such as No More Deaths, a coalition of faith and community groups providing direct aid to migrants, saving their lives in the barren desert. Hundreds of migrants perish each year in an attempt to cross the desert and seek refuge in the United States.

The group also met with ICE agents, a much different tactic than Mijente's strategy. Beth noticed that many ICE agents had entered the field with the idea that they would be pursuing noble missions of keeping Americans safe and preventing dangerous criminals from entering the country. But their daily work didn't conform to the mission they had in mind.

"They basically went into it thinking they were going to be stopping bad guys," said Beth. "They're gonna stop the drug smugglers. Instead they're dealing with a humanitarian crisis, and they're not equipped for it."

Both Beth and Mijente leaders addressed the fact that immigration missteps transcend political parties. Beth pointed out that the Trump administration may have been an accelerant with his malicious policies of family separation, but harsh immigration practices have persisted in Democratic administrations under Clinton and Obama too. Mijente's Camp Compasión was destroyed with the blessing of Louisville's Democratic mayor. Defeating a politician like Trump didn't mean a perpetual victory for immigration advocacy.

Although the zero tolerance policy was revoked after tremendous public pressure and lawsuits, some of the harsh immigration tactics persist and have made their way into statehouses across the country.

The Kentucky House took up a bill in 2021 that could easily lead to family separation and leave Kentuckians vulnerable to racial profiling and intimidation. House Bill 242 aimed to ban sanctuary cities, withhold funding from any municipality daring to operate as a sanctuary city, prohibit universities from accepting undocumented students, and mandate that universities keep records of students' immigration status, among other things.

Even in a Republican-controlled General Assembly, the bill died. But the ACLU of Kentucky, which strongly opposed the bill, didn't take too much time to celebrate its defeat. They warn that the Kentucky Senate has similar priorities and they fully expect similar bills to be introduced in the future.

In the early twentieth century, immigrants left their home countries to work at Appalachian coal mines in Hazard and other eastern Kentucky towns. Today the commonwealth has slightly fewer immigrants than other states, with immigrants making up only 4 percent of the population. But the number has been steadily growing through the years.

Opponents of immigration often bark complaints about the economic impact, sharing myths that migrants are going to be draining welfare services, and raising the nonsensical prospect of migrants both taking jobs from Americans and leeching unemployment benefits as if they're a golden ticket. But in fact the 160,000 foreign-born Kentuckians have collectively made an extremely positive economic impact.

Thousands of Kentuckian immigrants are entrepreneurs who in turn employ thousands of Kentuckians. Over the course of one year, the immigrant population of Kentucky earned nearly $4 billion, which sent more than $343 million to state and local tax coffers alone. Undocumented Kentuckians earned $748.9 million and—yup—they pay taxes too. So Kentucky and local municipalities received $56.8 million from the undocumented population.

Just as they arrived at the Appalachian coal mines a century ago, immigrants come to Kentucky today with the same goal—they're ready to work. According to a report by New American Economy, immigrants were 37 percent more likely to work than native-born Kentuckians. They're also more likely to hold graduate degrees. They buy homes and boost the housing market. They create and retain jobs. Perhaps there is a grain of validity in the MAGA enthusiasts' insecurity. Immigrants are getting the job done in industries from manufacturing to STEM in a way native Kentuckians simply have not.

Outside the economic impact, Kentucky's immigrant and undocumented population have revitalized rural areas otherwise considered neglected. For anyone challenging the idea that diversity is our strength, I must remind you that not long ago our taco options were limited to Tumbleweed or Taco Bell. Now you can get authentic Mexican food in Hazard between the flea market and Tractor's Supply.

Diversify Your Activism

- Be bold like Mijente. Recognize the types of actions that engage others and bring attention to vital issues.

- Be mindful of your biases. Stick to the convictions that matter most to you, and hold political leaders, regardless of party, accountable.
- Bear witness like Beth and never let anyone deny what you saw with your own eyes.
- Hold on to cautious optimism like the ACLU of Kentucky. Stay focused on the issues affecting Kentuckians now, but be prepared for future battles.
- Allow the lived experiences of new Kentuckians, their resilience, and their dreams to inspire you.

NINE

FEMINISM AND REPRODUCTIVE RIGHTS

ONE OF THE MOST prolific feminist thinkers of our time, Gloria Jean Watkins, was adamant that her identity not distract from her message. She borrowed her pen name "bell hooks" from her grandmother, Bell Blair Hooks, and styled it lowercase to keep the reader's attention on her words, but not necessarily on her. Yet her identity and Kentucky heritage enlightened the feminist thought she pioneered, which feels more relevant than ever in the wake of her death in late 2021.

Watkins was born in segregated Hopkinsville, Kentucky, in the 1950s to a Black working-class family. The town was subject to the practice of "blockbusting," as real estate agents used fearmongering tactics, telling white residents that Blacks would soon be moving in, to convince them to sell their houses at a significant discount. Then the real estate agents would sell those homes at inflated prices to Black families desperate for affordable housing. Today the town remains one of the most segregated in Kentucky, right behind Louisville.

A natural academic from the start, Watkins thrived in the all-Black school she attended, which she described as "sheer joy." She believed the Black women teaching wanted their students to forge new identities as scholars and thinkers. She loved to learn, and it seemed her teachers loved that about her and wanted that for all their students. Within the walls of a classroom, Watkins felt empowered to reinvent herself and explore new ideas, thriving on the encouragement from her teachers. Through this nurturing of critical thinking, she identified her eventual calling of being a writer and teacher herself.

When schools became integrated, she was bused to a school of white students and faculty. She hated it. The focus of learning in this school was to memorize and learn facts and information that felt irrelevant to who she was and what she was interested in. Instead of students being encouraged to think freely, they were taught to be obedient.

Always brilliant and academically skilled, Watkins thrived enough in school to win a scholarship to Stanford University, where she earned her Bachelor of Arts in English. Then she went on to also earn a Master of Arts in English at the University of Wisconsin–Madison. She taught and wrote, just as she was always called to do, and then finished her doctorate in literature at the University of California, Santa Cruz.

While she studied at Stanford, she took Women's Studies courses and, along with the other women in the class, was energized by the passion of the ongoing women's activism spilling over into the curriculum. But she also noticed someone was missing from the conversation about women's rights—Black women.

At only nineteen she began writing her first book, *Ain't I a Woman: Black Women and Feminism*, heavily influenced by this fresh experience. She wrote out of necessity.

A book fully exploring a Black woman's identity as well as how this fits into the modern feminist movement didn't exist, so she had to write it herself. She saw her reality as a Black woman to be unique, utterly distinct from white women, even if they were fighting for women's equality, and from both white and Black men.

She pioneered ideas in *Ain't I a Woman* that are frequently discussed today in Kentucky social justice groups fighting for racial equity, like Black Lives Matter Louisville. She discussed the overall disregard of issues of race and class within the fight for women's rights. She called out how Black women specifically had been left out of conversations. She introduced the idea of a white supremacist capitalist patriarchy.

She introduced this "white supremacist capitalist patriarchy" concept because she wanted to explore in a digestible way how the systems that oppress are related and work together as one. She believed if you want to truly examine the source of oppression, you have to also consider these intersections. So if you're a Black woman and, because you feel you're being oppressed by racist influences, you embrace the goal of dismantling white supremacy, you also have to consider capitalism and patriarchy. For Watkins, they all work together.

This is the lens through which many Kentuckians advocating for the end of white supremacy approach the issue. When I talk to someone in the Kentucky Alliance Against Racist and Political Repression, some members' socialist ideas are shared. When I see what events Change Today, Change Tomorrow is hosting, they're focused on mutual aid for people suffering in the toils of capitalism. The experiences of Black women are not lumped in with the experiences of white women, they're recognized as the extremely different experiences they are. So many change makers in Kentucky are not focused on dismantling one thing; they refer to themselves as abolitionists focused on tearing down the whole system that allows oppression of anyone to thrive. Feminism must be intersectional or it's worthless.

Watkins understood that the harm inflicted on Black people was not only due to blatant racist acts that white people committed, it was also the entire system of white supremacy that made white the default and pushed Black to the margins. She credits growing up in heavily segregated Hopkinsville for giving her the ability to recognize the underlying factors that allow white supremacy to thrive. In preferring to speak of white supremacy rather than racism, she believed issues like colonization and internalized racism could be properly addressed.

Influenced by the works of Sojourner Truth (whose "Ain't I a Woman?" speech inspired the title of her first book), James Baldwin, Malcolm X, and Dr. Martin Luther King Jr., she never stopped learning, writing, thinking, and teaching. She wrote a new book almost every year exploring revolutionary feminist theory, race, class, education, and media.

Watkins returned to Kentucky in 2004 to join Berea College as a Distinguished Professor in Residence in Appalachian Studies. She joined local feminist thinkers, some new to exploring their own ideas and some with well-established theories, in weekly discussion groups called Monday Night Feminism and an afternoon luncheon lecture series called Peanut Butter and Gender.

Feminism must be intersectional or it's worthless.

She decided to make her permanent home in Kentucky once more, establishing herself in Berea and founding the bell hooks institute at Berea College. The institute at the college, which does not charge tuition, for Watkins is a way to protect her legacy.

After she decided to move back to Kentucky, she published *Belonging: A Culture of Place*, which included conversation with fellow Kentucky writer Wendell Berry. Here's a bit from the chapter "Kentucky Is My Fate."

If one has chosen to live mindfully, then choosing a place to die is as vital as choosing where and how to live. Choosing to return to the land and landscape of my childhood, the world of my Kentucky upbringing, I am comforted by the knowledge that I could die here. This is the way I imagine "the end": I close my eyes and see hands holding a Chinese red lacquer bowl, walking to the top of the Kentucky hill I call my own, scattering my remains as though they are seed and not ash, a burnt offering on solid ground vulnerable to the wind and rain—all that is left of my body gone, my being shifted, passed away, moving forward on and into eternity. I imagine this farewell scene and it solaces me; Kentucky hills were where my life began. They represent the place of promise and possibility and the location of all my terrors, the monsters that follow me and haunt my dreams. Freely roaming Kentucky hills in childhood, running from snakes and all forbidden outside terrors both real and imaginary, I learn to be safe in the knowledge that facing what I fear and moving beyond it will keep me secure. With this knowledge I nurtured a sublime trust in the power of nature to seduce, excite, delight, and solace.

The Battle for Reproductive Justice

After legal challenges and restrictive laws pushed by lawmakers hell-bent on ending abortion in the commonwealth, only one abortion clinic is left standing in downtown Louisville and only two in the commonwealth as of this writing. Every Saturday morning, as the few patients arrive at the clinic for the procedure, dozens of protestors are there to greet them.

The protestors, who call themselves sidewalk counselors, hold gruesome signs portraying what they claim is an aborted fetus, they chant, they pray, and when a patient arrives, they surround the woman and, during her brief walk to the door, desperately try to persuade her not to have the procedure.

Volunteers passionate about reproductive justice, who serve as "clinic escorts" wearing bright, fluorescent vests, ask the patient if she would like guidance to exactly where she needs to go. If so, the escorts will shield the patient from the protestors with their bodies and guide her into the clinic. They also watch for patients due to arrive, so they don't accidentally go to the fake clinic.

The . . . fake . . . what?

Oh, yeah. Right beside the abortion clinic, there is another facility formerly called A Woman's Choice and now called BsideU. The building looks exactly the way you might think an abortion provider would look. In the logo, a straight line beneath "BsideU" leads to the jagged indications of a heartbeat and then to the words "for life." When the clinic rebranded, Governor Matt Bevin, a strong opponent of abortion who had been successful in restricting it in Kentucky, attended the ribbon cutting ceremony, saying, "I don't understand. Who's against life?"

On the BsideU website, the home page until recently featured a young woman looking overwhelmed, sitting on the floor, back against the wall, looking at the pregnancy test in her hand. The text beside her read,

"Pregnant? Not sure what to do or where to go? We can help." Now the message is much the same, but its background toggles between photos of two young women, a blonde and a brunette, both smiling inexplicably broadly.

The website shares pregnancy information including the "baby's stages of development" and little tidbits such as that fingernails start to appear between nine and twelve weeks of gestation. But the fun facts and stages of development actually stop at twenty weeks, so the information is relevant only for the stages in which abortion is legally possible. It's subtle hints like these that might suggest to a potential patient that this is not a women's healthcare provider, although the center claims to provide medical services.

As far as abortion information is concerned, the website declares, "We know some choices are harder than others. We're here to help you." They claim if you stop by, they can perform a pregnancy test to confirm the pregnancy, determine gestational age, educate patients about the different abortion procedures, and—most important for the mission of BsideU—educate the patient about alternatives. If someone has had an abortion, the group offers to help guide the woman to healing though Christianity and claims it's common to grapple with depression, regret, and suicidal impulses after abortion. (That might give pause to a patient considering abortion, no?)

The façade of the building, its proximity to an actual abortion clinic, and its vague language are all meant to get a pregnant patient who is considering abortion through their door. It's confusing by design. While there are only two abortion clinics in the entire commonwealth, there are forty-nine crisis pregnancy centers. Similar in design to BsideU, they're found both in rural areas and in cities such as Louisville, Lexington, and Shelbyville. They also have names suggesting they merely offer healthcare services to women, such as Pregnancy Support Center in Bowling Green, AA Women's Services in Corbin, and Appalachian Pregnancy Care Center in Pikeville.

The Kentucky Health Justice Network (KHJN) is a bit more forward with its beliefs and mission—the organization believes reproductive rights are human rights and Kentuckians must be allowed to decide if, when, and how to parent. The KHJN aims to improve access through direct action, funding abortion services for those unable to afford them. (One escort likes to take selfies with extra-vocal antiabortion activists and use the photos to solicit abortion funds.)

The KHJN also strives to provide necessary funds and access for transgender Kentuckians. Its Trans Health Advocacy program helps link trans patients with LGBTQ-friendly healthcare providers, financial assistance for gender-affirming care, and community resources they might find beneficial.

In 2009 I covered the ongoing battle between anti-abortion advocates and pro-choice clinic escorts for Louisville's alternative weekly, *LEO*. It was shortly after the Stupak Amendment passed, preventing federal funds from being used for health insurance that includes abortion coverage. There were two clinics in the commonwealth providing abortions at the time. I went to the Louisville EMW clinic, which regularly had a crowd of protestors on the sidewalks.

For much of the day, antiabortion protestors clutched their crosses and fetus signs beside children kneeling while clinic escorts stood closer to the clinic doors rolling their eyes and making small talk. Throughout the entire day— at the time, one of only two days abortions were performed each week—few patients arrived. But when they did, it was like Kim Kardashian sneaking out of the Met Gala.

The patient was quickly introduced to clinic escorts, who explained they were there to take her to the clinic doors and shield her from the protestors, if she'd like. I did not witness one patient decline this offer. The escorts swiftly walked the patients to the clinic doors while protestors swarmed around them doing everything they felt they could in that brief moment to coax the patients not to enter the doors. They screamed at the patients not to murder their babies and begged them to allow someone else to raise them, saying that God had a plan for their babies.

Then the patients walked in the doors for the procedure and everyone took a breath.

Almost every abortion provider across the country has a picketing presence outside the clinic. In the Midwest and South, the protestors are especially aggressive compared to the rest of the country. One study involving women across the United States who have had abortions examined the emotional effect the protests have on them, because women who are harassed on the way into the clinic still go on to have the procedure. Roughly half of the patients surveyed confirmed they saw and heard protestors and were upset by them. Sixteen percent reported feeling extremely upset. Then, one week later, they were generally feeling fine, no longer upset by the experience inflicted upon them by protestors.

Studies have not shown women to have been successfully persuaded by the antiabortion protestors. Believe it or not, damning a patient to Hell and calling her a murderer isn't the convincing argument protestors believe it is. The protestors are successful in upsetting women, but even that emotional response fades. The harassment, which bothers the patient for approximately thirty seconds, is effective mostly in annoying the clinic escorts, who become as familiar with the protestors as you might with a coworker.

When I observed the protests, I felt deeply uncomfortable. Like many women in their early twenties, I had a strong fear of confrontation. I had a difficult time holding a conversation with protestors and not allowing myself to be distracted by the dismembered fetus on the signs they were holding. I couldn't match the energy of a jolly clinic escort, who was visibly unfazed by the protestor making the sign of the cross and rocking behind her. But within this chaotic moral battle, there was camaraderie.

One clinic escort said he had shown up every week for years to support a women's right to choose, and he could sum up the reasons in three words—compassion, mercy, and charity. But he was quick to point out that these reasons were likely the same for the protestors. It's simply that the clinic escorts are focused on the patient and the protestors are focused on the unborn fetus. As he told me this, a protestor behind him packed up his fetus posters and yelled to him, "See you next week!" The escort shouted back, "See you next week, buddy."

A decade later, when the EMW clinic had become the only abortion provider remaining in the commonwealth, the moral battle continued to rage outside but the camaraderie seemed to have faded.

For years, reproductive choice advocates had been demanding a buffer zone around the clinic. Protestors were becoming increasingly brazen, harassing patients in close proximity. Many patients reported protestors touching them and physically blocking their access to the clinic doors. Local police frequently had to respond to conflicts between protestors and patients as tensions rose and personal boundaries were broken.

Louisville Metro Council member Jecorey Arthur, a supporter of the buffer zone, said, "One thousand four hundred and thirty-one incidents on this sidewalk in your downtown Louisville. That's a very unsafe sidewalk."

Legally, the protestors have the right to express themselves, which includes yelling at patients on the sidewalk and holding nightmarish signs. Likewise, the clinic escorts have the right to wear "Abortion is normal" gear and make as many snarky comments as they wish. But no one has the right to interfere with the patients physically entering the clinic or to touch each other without consent.

The buffer zone was proposed out of concern for public safety, and not just on behalf of the patients and clinic escorts. In 2019 a female protestor approached a patient with literature advertising the crisis pregnancy center, exhorting her not to terminate. The patient angrily accosted her in return, and the eighty-two-year-old protestor, standing five-foot-two and weighing 108 pounds, fell to the concrete ground. The elderly protestor broke her femur and required surgery.

From a distance of ten feet away, protestors can still express their messages, and the patients can hear and see them. A buffer zone doesn't prevent protests, and courts have established that it's not an infringement on First Amendment rights, which can still be exercised from ten feet away.

After much debate and controversy over the necessity of a buffer zone, reproductive justice advocates could celebrate a rare victory in the commonwealth. An ordinance establishing the buffer zone they'd long proposed was officially adopted by the Louisville Metro Council in early 2021.

The war over reproductive rights continues to rage in Kentucky, with battles being won and lost on either side. Just during the writing of this book, Kentucky went from one abortion provider in the commonwealth to two. Organizations like the Kentucky Health Justice Network continue to expand and offer more services, such as gender affirming care for trans patients.

The website www.canIgetanabortioninKentucky.com is constantly updated with new information as clinics close and open, policies change, and the threat of *Roe v. Wade* being overturned looms in the federal sphere. But the answer to the question "Can I get an abortion in Kentucky?" has remained yes, and there's a battalion of advocates fighting to keep it that way.

Protect Women's Rights as Human Rights in the Commonwealth

- Learn from Kentucky's homegrown feminist theorist Gloria Jean Watkins a.k.a. bell hooks and make sure the feminism you practice is truly intersectional and for everyone.

- Recognize the unique experiences other Kentuckians face, and allow them to lead the movements.
- Be as tenacious as the reproductive justice advocates who have suffered many losses but keep fighting and ultimately, in their minds, win every day a woman is trusted with decisions regarding her own body.
- Understand, as bell hooks taught, that big, systemic issues involve oppressive systems working together. If you want to dismantle the system, attack each piece.
- Honor the legacies of Kentucky activists as bell hooks wished, treat them as seeds to be planted, and allow them to flourish and grow into something beautiful together.

ACKNOWLEDGMENTS

I HAVE a tremendous amount of gratitude for the Kentuckians I spoke with in writing this book. I truly feel so inspired by your stories and honored by the opportunity to share them. Thank you all for the relentless work you do to make Kentucky a better place for everyone. Thank you to my family, my husband Patrick and children Daniel and Penelope, for your loving support. I know preschoolers and second-graders don't always appreciate when Mommy has a deadline, and I cherish your patience and understanding beyond your years. Patrick, as always, I love you and am grateful to have you as my constant cheerleader. Thank you to my parents for encouraging me to fight for what I believe is right and just.

Thank you to my brilliant agent, Alice. I am so fortunate to have such a ferocious champion for my work, and I'm endlessly grateful for your expertise and kindness.

Thank you to Patrick O'Dowd for your editorial prowess, your friendly conversation, and most of all your infectious enthusiasm for this book and highlighting the many beautiful things about Kentucky.

Thank you to Ashley Runyon for your creative vision and to everyone at University Press of Kentucky for showing that Kentucky is much more than a bucket of fried chicken.

Thank you for reading. Take the lessons you've learned from these incredible Kentuckians and keep fighting.

SOURCE NOTES

1. Poverty

"These Are the 25 Worst Counties to Live In. Did Yours Make the List?" by Samuel Stebbins and Michael B. Salter, in *USA Today*, March 13, 2019, with a picture gallery, is at www.usatoday.com/story/money/2019/03/13/worst-places-live-us-counties-ranked-poverty-life-expectancy/39163929/.

Statistics about poverty in Kentucky compared to the rest of the Appalachian region are drawn from Federation of Appalachian Housing Enterprises, "Poverty in Appalachia," fahe.org/appalachian-poverty/.

Data about coal mining job losses are drawn from Robert Pauley, "Alpha Natural Resources to Close Last Kentucky Mine," CBS FOX 59, September

12, 2016, www.wvnstv.com/archives/alpha-natural-resources-to-close-last-kentucky-mine/.

Conversation with Ben Carter occurred via Zoom on February 23, 2021.

"There's a part of Kentucky . . ." quotes Benjamin Jones, *Wallins Creek: An American Town Nestled in Southeast Kentucky* (2021).

Accounts of food disparity throughout Louisville are drawn from Shauntrice Martin's *The Bok Choy Project*, available through the Root Cause Research Center at www.rootcauseresearch.org/post/the-bok-choy-project-by-shauntrice-martin.

Quotations representing Kroger are drawn from an email interview with Erin Grant, Corporate Affairs Manager and Media Relations, conducted by the author on March 16, 2021.

Conversation with Taylor Ryan occurred via Zoom on January 16, 2021.

2. Environment

Conversation with Craig Williams occurred via Google Meet on February 23, 2021.

Redlining is explored in Anne Marshall, "Dividing Lines: Redlining in Louisville," *Louisville Magazine*, March 2017, www.louisville.com /redlining-louisville-dividing-lines/.

Information regarding cancer risk of Rubbertown residents is drawn from Erica Peterson's nine-part *Rubbertown and Health: The Whole Series*, which aired on WFPL in January 2021 and may be found at wfpl.org/ rubbertown-and-health-whole-series-0/.

3. Religion

Accounts of the June 1, 2020, protests are drawn from the *New York Times*'s video analysis of the David McAtee shooting, nytimes.com/video/us/100000007175316/the-david-mcatee-shooting-did-aggressive-policing-lead-to-a-fatal-outcome.html, and especially from Kala Kachmar, "Minute by Minute: What Happened the Night David McAtee Was Shot Dead by National Guard," *Louisville Courier Journal*, June 18, 2020, www.courier-journal.com/in-depth/news/crime/2020/06/18/what-happened-david-mcatee-shooting-in-west-end-louisville-kentucky/5333734002/.

Quotations of Representative Attica Scott are drawn from a Google Meet interview conducted by the author on March 1, 2021.

Account of the September 24, 2020, protests is drawn from Claire Galofaro, "Inside the Church at the Heart of the Louisville Protests," Associated Press, October 1, 2020, apnews.com/article/breonna-taylor-race-and-ethnicity-louisville-archive-9abb9025e6fa8080de5d0cf0d817d1bf.

Quotations of Ben Carter are drawn from the Zoom conversation on February 23, 2021.

Quotations of Pam McMichael are drawn from a Google Meet interview conducted by the author on March 11, 2021.

Conversation with Ira Grupper occurred via Zoom on March 9, 2021.

Details on the jailing of protestors in Mississippi are drawn from the Civil Rights Digital Library, especially the collection False Witness from the Mississippi State Sovereignty Commission, November 1965–January 1966, at crdl.usg.edu/export/html/mus/sovcomfolders/crdl_mus_sovcomfolders_99-73-0.html?Welcome.

4. Education

Accounts of Matt Bevin's comments regarding the teacher protests are drawn from the *Louisville Courier Journal*, especially from Mandy McLaren and Lucas Aulbach, "Bevin: Children Were Sexually Assaulted and Tried Drugs Because Teachers Were Protesting," April 13, 2018, and a televised interview with Bevin on WKYT's *Kentucky Newsmakers* in June 2019.

Quotations of Brandy Brewer are drawn from a telephone conversation on May 4, 2021.

Quotation of Richard L. Witherlite is from Peter T. Kilborn, "Kentucky Steps Up Fight on Illiteracy," *New York Times*, July 27, 2000.

5. Political Representation

Conversation with Representative Attica Scott occurred via Zoom on March 1, 2021.

Information regarding the Hood to the Holler initiative is drawn from its website hoodtotheholler.org.

Quotation of H. R. Haldeman is from the Monday, April 28, 1969, entry of *The Haldeman Diaries: Inside the Nixon White House* (New York: G. P. Putnam's Sons, 1994).

Quotations of Ben Carter are drawn from the Zoom conversation on February 23, 2021.

Conversation with Tayna Fogle and Pam McMichael occurred via Google Meet on March 11, 2021.

6. Racial Justice

Quotes of Alberta Jones are drawn from "Hard to Keep Up With, That's Alberta Jones," *Louisville Courier Journal*, March 4, 1965.

Accounts of the September 23, 2020, protests are drawn from live reporting on Twitter by WFPL's Ryan Van Velzer.

Accounts of the 1969 Kentucky Derby protests are drawn from Emily Bingham, "A Race about Race," *Louisville Magazine*, April 2019.

Accounts of Breonna Taylor's killing are drawn from the *New York Times*, especially Malachy Browne, Anjali Singhvi, Natalie Reneau, and Drew Jordan, "How the Police Killed Breonna Taylor," December 28, 2020, www.nytimes.com/video/us/100000007348445/breonna-taylor-death-cops.html, and the *Louisville Courier Journal*, especially Tessa Duvall, "Breonna Taylor Shooting: A Minute-by-Minute Timeline of the Events That Led to Her Death," September 23, 2020, www.courier-journal.com/story/news/local/breonna-taylor/2020/09/23/minute-by-minute-timeline-breonna-taylor-shooting/3467112001/.

Further accounts of the protests in downtown Louisville in response to Breonna Taylor's killing are drawn from the author's personal experience.

7. LGBTQ+ Rights

Conversation with Paul Campion occurred via email in March 2021.

Account of Jeffrey Wasson's 1986 legal battle is drawn from the case *Kentucky v. Wasson*.

Conversation with Dan Canon occurred via email in March 2021.

Conversation with Sister Petty Davis occurred via Facebook in March 2021.

8. Immigration

Accounts of the Occupy ICE protests are drawn from the *Louisville Courier Journal*, WHAS 11, and WFPL coverage in July 2018.

For the full Elie Wiesel speech, see israelforever.org/interact/blog/elie_wiesel_bearing_witness/.

Conversation with Beth Salamon occurred by telephone on May 4, 2021.

9. Feminism and Reproductive Rights

Quotation of Council member Jecorey Arthur is drawn from a Louisville Metro Council meeting held on May 20, 2021.

Accounts of the altercation outside the EMW clinic are drawn from the *Louisville Courier Journal*.

SUGGESTED READING

For each of the topics covered in this book, there is a seemingly endless abundance of information. Such a plethora of resources can feel overwhelming, so I gathered some of the best books most applicable to Kentuckians interested in deepening their political activism in one of the covered areas. Happy reading!

1. Poverty

In the ultimate Appalachian hate-read, *Hillbilly Elegy*, J. D. Vance tells the story of how he broke the cycle of poverty, addiction, and dysfunction that his rural Kentucky family was otherwise doomed to continue. In spite of them, he became an outlier, an Ivy League–educated attorney, and an occasional Fox News guest. In *Hill Women: Finding Family and a Way Forward in the Appalachian Mountains*, Cassie Chambers shares her story of generational poverty in rural Kentucky and relates how these experiences led her too to become an Ivy League–educated attorney. But Chambers's story is one of tremendous pride, not spite, and she credits these "hill women" values of generosity, passion, and strength as guiding forces in her life. She addresses issues many poor women in rural Kentucky face, such as opioid addiction and domestic violence, and breaks down the systematic causes that contribute to those issues instead of overgeneralizing a mythical hillbilly monolith.

Cassie Chambers, *Hill Women: Finding Family and a Way Forward in the Appalachian Mountains* (New York: Ballantine Books, 2020)

2. Environment

Many of beloved author Wendell Berry's works read like love letters to Kentucky, a place he has chosen to make his home and his fate. In *The Unsettling of America: Culture and Agriculture*, Berry examines how the evolution to industrial agriculture from small farming impacts our economy, health, and communities. The book holds its relevance even decades after it was first written and is a great primer for understanding environmental issues in the commonwealth.

Wendell Berry, *The Unsettling of America: Culture and Agriculture* (San Francisco: Sierra Club, 1977; reprint, Berkeley, CA: Counterpoint, 2004)

In *Something's Rising: Appalachians Fighting Mountaintop Removal*, authors Silas House and Jason Howard share oral histories of Central Appalachians who have endured the consequences of mountaintop removal. The destructive process, used by the coal industry as an alternative to strip mining, not only destroys the ecological wonder making up the mountainous landscape but pollutes waterways and endangers the health of nearby communities. The inspirational accounts from activists show how detriment to our environment affects real lives.

Silas House and Jason Howard, *Something's Rising: Appalachians Fighting Mountaintop Removal* (Lexington: University Press of Kentucky, 2009)

3. Religion

Kentucky pastor Guthrie Graves-Fitzsimmons rejects the notion that progressive values and Christianity cannot coexist. In his book *Just Faith: Reclaiming Progressive Christianity*, Graves-Fitzsimmons makes the case that progressive Christians are not a fringe group, they're the majority. Huge majorities of American Christians support marriage equality and reproductive justice. Yet the loudest Christians seem to be the ones citing their religious beliefs while harassing women outside abortion clinics and refusing services to the LGBTQ+ community. Graves-Fitzsimmons points out that some of the most celebrated activists, such as Dr. Martin Luther King Jr., were driven by their faith to take on the righteous fight for civil rights. Progressive Christian activists continue that tradition, and their stories are at the forefront of *Just Faith*.

Guthrie Graves-Fitzsimmons, *Just Faith: Reclaiming Progressive Christianity* (Minneapolis: Broadleaf Books, 2020)

4. Education

Although far from the commonwealth, Tara Westover tells a story that could easily have taken place in rural Kentucky. Isolated in the mountains, Westover was raised by survivalists who didn't provide access to any type of formal education. She stepped foot in a classroom for the first time at age seventeen and went on to earn a PhD from Cambridge. This late-bloomer education enlightened her sheltered worldview and illuminates why education is so vital in society. With no schooling, she knew nothing of major historical events such as the Holocaust and was limited to seeing the world through the lens of her family's narrative. This empowering story provides a great perspective for education activists to keep up the fight.

Tara Westover, *Educated: A Memoir* (New York: Random House, 2018)

5. Political Representation

As Representative Attica Scott advised, if you want the Kentucky General Assembly to represent your interests, be more diverse, and look more like *all* the people they're elected to serve, you need to run for office. Pursuing a political office may not be as daunting as it sounds, but of course you need guidance. In *Run for Something: A Real-Talk Guide to Fixing the System Yourself*, author Amanda Litman provides practical and direct guidance to running for office. She correctly asserts that public office should not be an elite club reserved only for those with millions of disposable campaign dollars and/or Ivy League educations. What's even better about this guide is that the advice is applicable to down-ballot positions where the real-world magic happens—state legislatures, city councils, school boards, and mayoral races. This is a great guidebook if you have even a lukewarm interest in running for office, and it can help give you the tools you need to get started.

Amanda Litman, *Run for Something: A Real-Talk Guide to Fixing the System Yourself* (New York: Atria, 2017)

6. Racial Justice

Subversive Southerner dives deeper into Anne Braden's rejection of the Jim Crow status quo as it existed in Kentucky and the consequences she suffered after taking a stand for racial justice. But this is not a cautionary tale: the Bradens' legacy remains a relevant call to action. For white allies, this is a must read.

Catherine Fosl, *Subversive Southerner: Anne Braden and the Struggle for Racial Justice in the Cold War South* (New York: Palgrave Macmillan, 2002; reprint, Lexington: University Press of Kentucky, 2006)

Kentucky poet laureate Crystal Wilkinson's *Perfect Black* is a collection of poetry and prose that beautifully captures her experience of growing up Black in Kentucky. Her story provides a necessary perspective into Black Appalachia and a reminder of the voices to be uplifted in the fight for racial justice.

Crystal Wilkinson, *Perfect Black* (Lexington: University Press of Kentucky, 2021)

7. LGBTQ+ Rights

Once a Mormon missionary, author Samantha Allen nurtured a fondness for the often overlooked and dismissed flyover country. Years later, as she embraced her identity as a transgender woman, her fondness for red states and the progressives calling them home never wavered. In *Real Queer America: LGBT Stories from Red States*, Allen highlights the vibrant LGBTQ+ communities thriving in seemingly unlikely places.

Samantha Allen, *Real Queer America: LGBT Stories from Red States* (New York: Little, Brown, 2019)

8. Immigration

Immigration has remained a divisive political topic, with proponents of open borders typically citing humanitarian interests and opponents often citing security concerns. But economist and free migration advocate Bryan Caplan introduces a novel argument for unrestricted immigration. He argues that open borders would result in tremendous economic benefits and even eliminate global poverty. Filled with well-researched information, it's presented in an accessible way with colorful illustrations and infographics fitting for the meme age. This is a great resource to perhaps challenge your own thoughts regarding open borders, or at least give you a fresh perspective to debate your misguided friends on Facebook.

Bryan Caplan, *Open Borders: The Science and Ethics of Immigration* (New York: First Second, 2019)

9. Feminism and Reproductive Rights

For budding and established feminists, bell hooks's work is an essential education. *Ain't I a Woman* is a fantastic example of her revolutionary exploration into the intersection of race and sex. Intersectionality is a necessary component of feminism, and for Kentucky feminists there's no one better to learn from than the native Kentuckian feminist pioneer.

bell hooks, *Ain't I a Woman: Black Women and Feminism*, 2nd ed. (New York: Routledge, 2015)

INDEX

abortion rights. *See* reproductive justice
Abrams, Stacey, 127
Abramson, Jerry, 55
ACLU, 184
ACLU of Kentucky, 209, 212
addiction, 129, 137, 239–40
adoption, 170–71
Agent Orange Act, 36, 40
Ain't I a Woman (hooks), 215–16, 218, 244
air pollution, 50–57; Louisville's Strategic Toxic Air Reduction, 56

Air Pollution Control Board, 50
Air Pollution Control District, 53
antiracism, 3, 65, 72, 81, 94, 111, 146, 164, 166, 175
anti-Semitism, 80, 87
Appalachian Studies, 218
Arthur, Jecorey, 227, 238

Babbitt, Ashli, 108
Baldwin, James, 15, 218
Barber, William, II, 138–39
bell hooks. *See* hooks, bell
Belonging: A Culture of Place (hooks), 219

Bend the Arc: Jewish Action
      Louisville, 84
Berry, Wendell, 219, 240
Beshear, Andy, 88, 96–99, 137,
      189
Bevin, Matt, 31, 87–98, 139, 184,
      221, 236
Biden, Joe, 127
Black Lives Matter, 66, 84–85, 160,
      196, 216
black lung disease, 6
Black-owned small businesses,
      30
Black Panther Party, 152–54
Black Student Union, 153–58
Blue Grass Chemical Agent
      Disposal Plant, 42–44
Bluegrass Literacy Project,
      104–7
Bok Choy Project, 20–25, 34, 234
Booker, Charles, 121–27, 141
Braden, Anne, 78, 80, 146–52,
      164–66, 242–43
Braden, Carl, 78, 146–52
Brewer, Brandy, 92, 236

Cameron, Daniel, 161
Campion, Paul, 170–73, 175, 190
cancer, lung, 52–53
Canon, Dan, 177–79, 183, 190,
      238

Carroll, Danny, 113
Carter, Ben, 11–16, 33, 68–70, 122,
      234–36
cash bail, 162–63
Change Today, Change Tomorrow,
      25–30, 66, 217; Umoka Project,
      28
chemical weapons, 36–43;
      disposal, 38, 44. *See also* Blue
      Grass Chemical Agent Disposal
      Plant
Christianity, 70, 113–14, 132,
      241
Churches of Christ, National
      Council of, 75
Churchill Downs, 27, 156, 162
Civil Rights Act of 1964, 73, 145
Clay, Henry, 2
coal mining, 5–13, 18, 49–50,
      89–90, 102–3, 233, 240; black
      lung disease, 6
Coleman, Louis, 54–57
communism, 150–51
coronavirus. *See* COVID-19
Courier Journal, 124, 145, 147, 151,
      235–37
COVID-19, 10–12, 14, 28, 68, 96,
      159

Davis, Angela, 80, 164
Davis, Kim, 182–85

Decode Project, 103–4, 110
democracy, 107, 127, 132, 134–35
Derby City Sisters, 187–91
disability rights, 13, 79–80

eastern Kentucky, 5–6, 9, 11,
    17–18, 33, 36, 111, 119, 210

Feed the West, 24–26, 33–34
First Amendment rights, 199,
    228
First Unitarian Church, 65–68,
    85
Fischer, Greg, 60, 199–201
Floyd, George, 83, 160
Fogle, Tayna, 128–41
food insecurity, 16–34, 53, 130,
    164

General Assembly, Kentucky,
    112–14, 119, 209, 242
gentrification, 158
Gerth, Tyler, 163
*Great Shark Hunt: Strange Tales
    from a Strange Time, The*
    (Thompson), 50
Grupper, Ira, 3, 71–82
gun violence, 121–22

Hamilton (musical), 97
Hankison, Brett, 63

Hood to the Holler, 121, 125, 127,
    236
hooks, bell, 18, 213–20, 229–30,
    244
housing justice, 2, 10, 12–13, 15–16,
    46–47, 70, 73, 148, 151–54
Hudson, Blaine, 156–58

Ibáñez, Jesús, 197
illiteracy, 99–109, 236
Injustice Square Park, 60, 163–64
Israel, 81

Jefferson County Public Schools,
    89, 92
Jim Crow laws, 126, 148
Johnson, Randy, 170–73, 175,
    190
Jones, Alberta, 144–46, 153, 165,
    237
Jones, Alex, 108–9
Jones, Benjamin, 18, 234
Judaism, 80–84, 204–5; Hillel, 83;
    Orthodox, 72; *tikkun olam*, 83,
    84; Yiddish, 82

Kennedy, Anthony, 179
Kentuckians for the
    Commonwealth, 134–35,
    137–38

Kentucky, eastern, 5–6, 9, 11, 17–18, 33, 36, 111, 119, 210

Kentucky Alliance Against Racist and Political Repression, 80, 164–65, 217

Kentucky Derby, 1, 156–57, 162, 237

Kentucky Environmental Foundation, 41–44

Kentucky Equal Justice Center, 12–16, 68, 122; Maxwell Street Legal Clinic, 13–14

Kentucky General Assembly, 112–14, 119, 209, 242

Kentucky Health Justice Network, 223, 229

Kentucky House of Representatives. *See* Kentucky General Assembly

Kentucky Supreme Court, 174

King, Martin Luther, Jr., 3, 84, 131–32, 144, 218, 241

Kroger, 20–24, 28, 32, 234

Kyle, Lori, 68

Lawrence v. Texas, 175, 179

Letter from Birmingham Jail (King), 3, 146

literacy. *See* illiteracy

LMPD. *See* Louisville Metro Police Department

Louisville, West, 19–25, 33, 46–47, 50, 61, 119, 154, 164

Louisville Metro Council, 227–29, 238

Louisville Metro Police Department, 63, 158–62, 199–201

lung cancer, 52–53

marriage equality, 65, 172–86

Martin, Shauntrice, 20–25, 33, 234

maternal mortality, 115–17

McAtee, David, 24, 61–62, 235

McCarthyism, 150

McConnell, Mitch, 2, 39–40, 44, 121–23, 125

McCreary County, Kentucky, 7, 10, 20–21

McGee, Willie, 148

McGrath, Amy, 123, 125

McMichael, Pam, 70–71, 131, 141, 235–36

Medicaid, 116, 139

medical debt, 15

Mijente Louisville, 196–201

mutual aid, 3, 16–19, 29, 33, 217

National Council of Churches of Christ, 75

National Guard, 24, 60–62

New York City, 72

Nixon, Richard, 126, 155–56, 236

Obergefell v. Hodges, 175–83

Palestine, 81

Pan-African Studies, 153, 155, 157–58

parenthood, 90, 171

Parrish-Wright, Shameka, 164–65

Parton, Dolly, 18

pay disparity, 115, 123, 134

Peterson, Erica, 52

Pike County, Kentucky, 9

police brutality, 59, 62, 74, 116, 153, 164

Poor People's Campaign, 70, 131–34, 138

Post, Suzy, 80

racial violence, 123

Reagan, Ronald, 156, 179

reproductive justice, 220–30, 241; abortion clinic buffer zone, 227–28

Roe v. Wade, 229

Rubbertown, 44–57

Rubbertown Emergency ACTion, 54

Ryan, Taylor, 3, 25–34, 66, 234

Salamon, Beth, 203–9

same-sex marriage. *See* marriage equality

Scott, Attica, 63–64, 114–21, 141, 235–36, 242

segregation, 47, 54, 72–73, 144–49

Singh, Tara, 106–7

Smoketown, 20, 54

Southern Poverty Law Center, 195

Strategic Toxic Air Reduction (Louisville), 56

Student Nonviolent Coordinating Committee, 3, 73

Supreme Court, Kentucky, 174

Supreme Court, United States, 149, 151, 170, 175, 177, 180, 184–85

Taylor, Breonna, 24, 59–60, 63, 80, 83–85, 112, 115, 117, 119, 143–63, 166–67

Thompson, Hunter S., 50–51

tikkun olam, 83, 84

trade unions, 147

transgender healthcare, 224

Trump, Donald, 96, 108, 193–96, 205–9

Umoka Project, 28

unemployment, 10, 69, 210

unions, 147

Until Freedom, 160–61

Vietnam War, 35–37, 40–41, 65; Agent Orange Act, 36, 40

voting rights, 131, 133–37, 140

Wade, Andrew, 148–51

Wade, Charlotte, 148–51

wage theft, 12–14

Walker, Kenneth, 159–60

Wall Between, The (Braden), 147

Wasson, Jeffrey, 173–75

Watkins, Gloria Jean. *See* hooks, bell

West Louisville, 19–25, 33, 46–47, 50, 61, 119, 154, 164

white flight, 50, 154

white supremacy, 81, 132, 216–17

Wiesel, Elie, 201–3

Williams, Craig, 35–44, 57

Women's March of 2017, 117

Women's Studies, 215

World War II, 38, 46, 48, 51, 205

Yiddish, 82

ABOUT THE AUTHOR

FARRAH ALEXANDER is a writer whose work focuses on feminism, parenting, social justice, politics, and current events. Her debut book, *Raising the Resistance: A Mother's Guide to Practical Activism,* is available now. As an advocate for gun reform, she is a member of the Everytown Authors Council, which was designed to "harness the power of the literary community to amplify the gun safety movement." She has also served as a Jeremiah Fellow with Bend the Arc: A Jewish Partnership for Justice, which aims to combat white supremacy and mobilize communities for social change. She currently serves on the Louisville Jewish Community Relations Council.

She holds a bachelor's degree from Indiana University and is currently pursuing a JD from that university's McKinney School of Law.

She lives outside Louisville, Kentucky, with her husband, son, and daughter.